7 Secrets
To The Mysteries Of
GOD

7 Secrets
To The Mysteries Of
GOD

A Guide For The Youth

Justin K Beekye

authorHOUSE®

AuthorHouse™
1663 Liberty Drive
Bloomington, IN 47403
www.authorhouse.com
Phone: 1-800-839-8640

First published by AuthorHouse   02/11/2012

ISBN: 978-1-4678-8460-0 (sc)
ISBN: 978-1-4678-8461-7 (ebk)

For Antoinette:
"The women who helped me reach my level"

How that by revelation He made known to me the mystery (as I have briefly written already, by which, when you read, you may understand my knowledge in the mystery of Christ)

(Ephesians 3:3-4)

CONTENTS

ACKNOWLEDGMENTS

I would first like to acknowledge the Creator of Heaven and Earth, to God who sent His only begotten Son to save mankind. Without the doing and the inspiration of Your Holy Scriptures, none would have been achieved.

Bishop Elisha Salifu Amoako, the General Overseer of Alive Chapel International, for the ongoing labor for the saints across the world. May God give you a double portion of what you already have.

To Rev Samuel Bentil and his beautiful wife, for watching over my soul day and night in an attempt to present a blameless young man before the end of time. My love is always for you.

To Rev Lawrence Larbie and his wonderful wife for the unending encouragement you have both shown in the past years and now. I wish you the very best in ministry.

INTRODUCTION

One of the most fundamental advice I often convey to God's people, is *"To know God for yourself—His glory, His power and His splendour"*.

Why would someone choose rather to know Him through another, when He has given us an invitation to have a personal relationship with Him through His Son Jesus Christ?

In my early years, I first understood God as being the '*Rule Man*'. If He had not spoken it, we had no right to quote it. A long while after, I discovered that men that left a remarkable blueprint throughout the bible, were in fact men that stood and done things which were dissimilar and uncommon. Such as:

- Abraham—Pleaded with God not to destroy Sodom & Gomorrah **(Genesis 18:23-33)**
- Moses—Convinced God not to destroy the Israelites **(Exodus 32:11-14)**
- Joshua—Commanded the sun to stand still **(Joshua 10:12-13)**

As a result, God had a unique thought towards these men.

- Abraham—The scriptures refer to him as '*the friend of God*' **(James 2:23)**
- Moses—God said *"I speak with him speak face to face"* **(Numbers 12:6-8)**
- Joshua—God '*heeded his voice*' and there has been no day like that, before it or after it **(Joshua 10:14)**

In time, Daniel revealed: *"But the people that do know their God shall be strong, and do exploits"* **(Daniel 11:32)** NIV.

In order for us to even begin the process of becoming strong and doing exploits, we first have to know God. Once you know God, the unknown will become known. I refer to this insight as being the secret key to everlasting success.

In closure, God has set aside a level for those whose minds are made up to attain the greater Christian experience which is divulged in my seven chapter book entitled '*The Seven Secrets to the Mysteries of God*'.

If men ask who we are, tell them *"Servants of Christ and Stewards of the mysteries of God"*.

Let a man so consider us, as servants of Christ and stewards of the mysteries of God.
                                                                          (1 Corinthians 4:1)

I invite you today to embark on a promising journey in discovering some of the greatest secrets to the mysteries of God.

CHAPTER 1

The Key to Answered Prayer

Then he said to me, "Do not fear, Daniel, for from the first day that you set your heart to understand, and to humble yourself before your God, your words were heard; and I have come because of your words.
– Daniel 10:12

Prayer can be described as a sold out, devoted, interactive communicational tool, in attempt to connect with a supreme being through words and expressions.

Looking at believers in Christ (*when praying*) it's very common to express prayer in a way of head bowed, crying, shouting, jumping, kneeling, standing etc. For the believer, there isn't a particular way.

The bible recalls Solomon praying in 1 Kings Chapter 8 on his knees.

When Solomon had finished all these prayers and supplications to the LORD, he rose from before the altar of the LORD, where he had been kneeling with his hands spread out towards heaven.
(1 Kings 8:54) NIV

There are many reasons why Christians find themselves praying to God. Some common examples are:

- To communicate with God
- Obeying God's command
- Honoring God
- In times of trouble
- Praying for others
- And many more . . .

Whatever the reason, God requires His people to pray to Him at all times.

Praying always with all prayer and supplication in the Spirit, being watchful to this end with all perseverance and supplication for all the saints.
(Ephesians 6:18)

The Experience . . .

Most Christians can identify with experiencing answered prayers as well as experiencing unanswered prayers.

Why do some prayers go unanswered whilst others go answered?

Often we assume unanswered prayers are as a result of sins committed in our life or maybe that particular prayer is not part of God's plan for us. However, in every prayer we release to the Father, we should first have an insight of what He thinks of it (*whether He is for it or against it*) even before we commit ourselves to praying on it. This is known as the will of God which we will touch on in a moment.

Firstly, we must understand it doesn't matter how many times we pray or fast to receive answers to our prayers. We need to know every decision is from the Lord and whatever the Lord says is final. The bible says, *"The lot is cast into the lap, but its every decision is from the LORD"* **(Proverbs 16:33)**.

Secondly, we need to be fully emerged in the will of God to receive answered prayers. Being fully emerged in the will of God, gives you the ability to glimpse the gifts that the Father has set aside for you in Heaven. For this reason, whenever you pray in accordance to what the Lord has already set aside for you, you're more than likely to receive answers to your prayers.

Now this is the confidence that we have in Him, that if we ask anything according to His will, He hears us. And if we know that He hears us, whatever we ask, we know that we have the petitions that we have asked of Him.

(1 John 5:14-15)

On the flip side, not being emerged in the will of God makes you short sighted. You will not be able to glimpse what gifts the Lord has for you, neither will you know the will of God. We just learnt, anything asked according to His will, He hears. So it's safe to say anything asked not according to His will may not be heard. In ignorance to His will, many may pray and become frustrated when this occurs. *"When you ask, you do not receive, because you ask with wrong motives, that you may spend what you get on your pleasures"* **(James 4:3) NIV**.

A time came when Jesus prayed and said, *"Father, if it is Your will, take this cup away from Me; nevertheless not My will, but Yours be done"* **(Luke 22:42)**. Jesus was simply saying if He could have His will, then it would be for the Father to take this cup away from Him, but later changed His prayer point heading back into the will of God and spoke saying, *"not My will but Yours be done"*.

We find our answers when we abide under His will. To enter into God's will, begin by giving thanks to Him in all circumstances no matter what it is, big or small—*"Give thanks in all circumstances, for this is God's will for you in Christ Jesus"* **(1 Thessalonians 5:18) NIV**.

Being in God's will, I understood that He intended to bless me at a very young age. I was able to receive every gift and blessing the Lord had prepared for me. Back in 1998, the word of the Lord came to me saying, *"I will bless you and allow you to speak my word to many, you will be married by the age of 25, and your first born will be a boy"*. I believed and stood on the promises of God, prayed and stayed in expectation to receive them according to the divine timing of the Lord.

Unto the glory of God, all this came to pass as the Lord had spoken.

The Growth . . .

Continuous prayer in all areas will expand and become a lifestyle, giving you unlimited access to receiving answered prayers. One of God's spiritual laws that operate here on earth is: *"For everyone who asks receives"* **(Matthew 7:8)**.

Also in the book of Mark it states . . .

I tell you the truth, if anyone says to this mountain, 'Go, throw yourself into the sea,' and does not doubt in his heart but believes that what he says will happen, it will be done for him. Therefore I tell you, whatever you ask for in prayer, believe that you have received it, and it will be yours.

(Mark 11:23-24) NIV

As you begin to grow in the Lord, God will expect you now to engulf in high performance prayers that will unlock great mysteries with the ability to change your circumstances. Apostle Paul pointed out the importance of growth in the scriptures.

"I gave you milk, not solid food, for you were not yet ready for it. Indeed, you are still not ready"

(1 Corinthians 3:2) NIV.

In this instance, milk can be described as a daily supplement given to newborns to enhance their growth. It is very much out of the norm to feed a newborn a piece of steak. The *'milk'* Apostle Paul spoke of was the Word of God. After close observation, Paul recognized that members of the Corinth church were operating at a lower spiritual level than expected, saying unto them *"you are still not ready"*. As a result, they missed out on a higher spiritual blessing Paul wanted to impart in their life. In the body of Christ it's important we grow daily in the Lord, as God can only deposit more to the growing and developing Christian rather than one who stays at the same level.

Apostle Paul spoke to the church in Philippians stating the procedure for receiving answered prayers: *"Do not be anxious about anything, but in everything, by prayer and petition, with thanksgiving, present your requests to God"* **(Philippians 4:6) NIV**.

A day came when the disciples of Jesus asked Him to teach them how to pray. Jesus responded by reciting to them what we know today to be Lord's Prayer **(Luke 11:2-4)**. However, Jesus went on to show them a small mystery on how to receive answered prayers by revealing to them a parable where a man went to his friend by midnight seeking food for a guest. The bible states, the friend inside the home told him the door is locked and his children were asleep. However, due to the man's boldness he received what he wanted.

Then he said to them, "Suppose one of you has a friend, and he goes to him at midnight and says, 'Friend, lend me three loaves of bread, because a friend of mine on a journey has come to me, and I have nothing to set before him.' "Then the one inside answers, 'Don't bother me. The door is already locked, and my children are with me in bed. I can't get up and give you anything.' I tell you, though he will not get up and give him the bread because he is his friend, yet because of the man's boldness he will get up and give him as much as he needs. "So I say to you: Ask and it will be given to you; seek and you will find; knock and the door will be opened to you. For everyone who asks receives; he who seeks finds; and to him who knocks, the door will be opened.

(Luke 11:5-9) NIV

I believe the man in the house with the children could be seen as an illustration of God in Heaven with His angels. The other man that was seeking bread could be seen as us. Notice the door was locked that contained the bread (answered prayer) and by no means was his petitions about to be answered by the man in his home with his children. But due to the man's boldness, Heavens gates were opened and answered prayers were released. **Hebrews 4:16** says "*Let us therefore come boldly to the throne of grace, that we may obtain mercy and find grace to help in time of need*".

When approaching God through prayer, let us remain humble but unto humbleness add boldness.

It is safe to say prayers are your direct phone call to God, an unlimited talk time He has granted us freely. But the secret of receiving answered prayers belongs to he who has an intimate relationship with the Lord.

Scriptural prayers are one of the most powerful tools to receiving answers to your prayers.

What does the bible say about this? Remember in the book of Isaiah when God spoke saying, "*Put Me in remembrance; Let us contend together; State your case, that you may be acquitted*" **(Isaiah 43:26)**. Isaiah was illustrating the nature of God. Reminding the Lord of what He had said concerning the matter will cause you to engage in a two way conversation with Him. In the book of Psalms the bible recalls: "*For You have magnified Your Word above all Your name*" **(Psalms 138:2)**.

Ezra a man of God had the ability to pray to God and receive many answered prayers. Ezra realized He had a unique gift from God which was to understand the scriptures (Law of Moses) in a deeper way than most men. As a result he was able to ask and receive much from the king as the Lord was always behind him.

This Ezra came up from Babylon. He was a teacher well versed in the Law of Moses, which the LORD, the God of Israel, had given. The king had granted him everything he asked, for the hand of the LORD his God was on him.

(Ezra 7:6) NIV

Daniel had a custom of praying three times a day. A custom he did from his early days.

Now when Daniel knew that the writing was signed, he went home. And in his upper room, with his windows open towards Jerusalem, he knelt down on his knees three times that day, and prayed and gave thanks before his God, as was his custom since early days.

(Daniel 6:10)

My belief is such; Daniel was the type of person who received answer prayers frequently. In **Daniel 1:8** we read how he purposed in his heart not to defile himself with the portion of the king's delicacies. In **Daniel 6:9-10**, the king signed a decree that no other god or man should be prayed to besides him for thirty days and many other trials and tribulations he endured for God. All of which could have easily made Daniel yield to the king's request, sin against God and then perhaps ask God for forgiveness at a later stage. But Daniel chose again rather to serve God than men. His determination, faithfulness and dependability to the King of Kings gave him the heavenly strength to fight the good fight of faith. No wonder why at the end of Daniel Chapter 12 it was said to Daniel: *"But you, go your way till the end; for you shall rest, and will arise to your inheritance at the end of the days"* **(Daniel 12:13)**.

We can learn so much from Daniel when studying this book, his secret to answered prayers. For Instance, take a look at what the Angel said to Daniel in Chapter 10.

And he said to me "O Daniel, man greatly beloved, understand the words that I speak to you, and stand upright, for I have now been sent to you," While he was speaking this word to me, I stood trembling. Then he said to me, "Do not fear, Daniel, for from the first day that you set your heart to understand, and to humble yourself before your God, your words were heard; and I have come because of your words".

(Daniel 10:11-12)

Only if we are able to set our heart in truth to understanding the things of God, and to humble ourselves before Him, we could experience answered prayers. We spoke about the physical law which works here on earth—*"For everyone who asks receives"*. I believe there is a spiritual law which works in heaven and when performed on earth releases Angelic help. That is, setting your heart to understanding and humbling yourself before God as Daniel did.

I found myself doing this in my early years of being a Christian, but never understood what I was lining myself up for. It suddenly dawned on me years after I came across this scripture which changed my life; and now I fully understood why I have been reaping the benefits of answered prayers.

At the age of 16, I was saved not quite having the firm understanding of my new life. I was still the head of a rap/street group called '*44 Chamberz*' (as it consisted of some 44 members including myself). However, my heart was different and I was unsatisfied. I remember saying to the Lord **"*I don't know where I am going or how far I can go in life; my dad had passed almost three years ago, but if by the age of 25 you could cause me to speak the revelations of Jesus in a discipleship way, married and established in my own business—then I too can say the Lord is with me.*"**

The Lord opened doors of opportunities in the year 2001. I began teaching my peers in college about the ways of Jesus. Many will come to learn as if they were attending classes. Some even skipped lunch to attend to the meetings. I just turned 18 at the time and had no understanding on receiving a message from the Lord; neither was I a member of a church let alone a *Spirit filled one*. So the Lord started waking me up every day at 6.00am for morning devotion and prayer for half an hour. I would then make my way downstairs to watch Creflo Dollar's World Changers broadcast, which aired at 6:30am (UK time). I began taking notes on his messages, what the title was, what he spoke about, and which scriptures he used. I would even throw in a few jokes that he used during his preaching service. I would take notes every single day for two and a half years before leaving for college each day. By lunch time in college, I would share Creflo's message to a growing audience. I had a reputation of being the '*nicest rapper*' around, with a body guard, and 44 unsaved thugs that moved with me from the 44 Chamberz. From what I can remember it created a spectacular infatuation that could never be missed. Students would ditch lunch to attend the meeting. They would see me walking through the court yard and will request to use the toilet just to see me.

The Attack . . .

Satan has the power to attack your prayers. Job said: "*let God weigh me in honest scales and he will know that I am blameless*" (**Job 31:6**) **NIV**.

If such a hedge is broken or open for whatever reason, Satan the accuser of the brethren, can hear your words, take your prayer and bury them causing you to never witness answered prayers. Many Christians believe when a prayer isn't answered it wasn't the will of God. In some cases this may be true, but in other cases, the enemy can hinder prayers.

A time came when Daniel experience the answers to his prayers being withstood by the enemy. Not for something he did, but for an illegal attack Satan was carrying out.

In **Daniel 10**, the Angel explained to Daniel that from the very first day he prayed he was sent to Daniel. But the Prince of Persia withstood him for twenty one days.

But the prince of the kingdom of Persia withstood me twenty-one days; and behold, Michael, one of the chief princes, came to help me, for I had been left alone there with the kings of Persia.

(Daniel 10:13)

Satan can also attack your prayers when he realizes that you as a Christian have a problem with someone else; whether through bitterness, unforgiving, hatred etc. This gives him legitimate rights to come in and block your prayers.

Therefore I say to you, whatever things you ask when you pray, believe that you receive them, and you will have them. "And when you stand praying, if you have anything against anyone, forgive him, so that your Father in heaven may also forgive you your trespasses. But if you do not forgive, neither will your Father in heaven forgive your trespasses."

(Mark 11:24-26)

Husbands, in the same way be considerate as you live with your wives, and treat them with respect as the weaker partner and as heirs with you of the gracious gift of life, so that nothing will hinder your prayers.

(1 Peter 3:7) NIV

Answered Prayer is based on your lifestyle

The Prophet Elijah made history when he prayed for no rain to fall on the earth. Was Elijah the only prophet in town at this time? Certainly not, the bible recalls in the book of 1 King 19-18 NIV *"Yet I reserve seven thousand in Israel-all whose knees have not bowed down to Baal and all whose mouths have not kissed him"*. So why couldn't any other Prophet call for the severe drought to stop? The relationship Elijah the Tishbite had with God was much more than the basic prophetic level, similar to how God related to Moses.

Hear now My words: If there is a prophet among you, I, the LORD, make Myself known to him in a vision; I speak to him in a dream. Not so with My servant Moses; He is faithful in all My house. I speak with him face to face, Even plainly, and not in dark sayings; And he sees the form of the LORD. Why then were you not afraid To speak against My servant Moses?"

(Numbers 12:6-8)

This shows us that God is able to do whatever He wants with whoever He wants to do it with.

A time came in the life of Elijah when he encountered the death of the widow's son. The bible says he prayed and God heard his voice.

"Then the LORD heard the voice of Elijah; and the soul of the child came back to him, and he revived"

(1 Kings 17:22)

There was something about Elijah that when he prayed, God heard his voice.

Elijah was a man with a nature like ours, and he prayed earnestly that it would not rain; and it did not rain on the land for three years and six months. And he prayed again, and the heaven gave rain, and the earth produce its fruit.

(James 5:17-18)

Never be put off or dismayed when waiting for answered prayers. If the Lord said it, He will surely do it. Remember the bible says in 2 Peter, *"The Lord is not slack concerning His promise, as some count slackness"* **(2 Peter 3:9)**.

Remember the story of Isaac and Rebekah. Isaac married beautiful Rebekah *(See Genesis 24:67)* and one day prayed on behalf of his wife for them to have children because she was barren. The bible says the Lord answered his prayer—*"Now Isaac pleaded with the Lord for his wife, because she was barren; and the Lord granted his plea, and Rebekah his wife conceived"* **(Genesis 25:21)**.

Isaac was forty years old when he took Rebekah as wife. God answered his prayers, and Isaac was sixty years old when Rebekah gave birth—"*Afterward his brother came out, and his hand took hold of Esau's heel; so his name was called Jacob. Isaac was sixty years old when she bore them*" **(Genesis 25:24-26)**.

Living a righteous life and being in tune with God all season round will attract God to your prayer. *"For the eyes of the Lord are on the righteous and his ears are attentive to their prayer, but the face of the Lord is against those who do evil"* **(1 Peter 3:12)**.

CHAPTER 2

Giving to the Poor and Needy

If a man shuts his ear to the poor, he too will cry out and not be answered.
—Proverbs 21:13

Definition of Poor—someone that is helpless, having little or no money, few possessions, lacking in specific resources, qualities or substances etc.

The poor could be seen as a needy person (someone in need). Being poor, often the picture illustrated is a homeless person (one who sleeps in the subways, public parks or even on high streets). We tend to feel compelled by what we see and would want to give a pound or two. Others wonder, *'how can I be sure this man really is poor?'* or *'how do I know he won't use my money to buy alcohol?'*—And many more questions . . .

The poor and needy extends broader than our perceptions. An example within a church environment could be a brother or a sister that is not employed, and as little as giving collections and offerings, one is unable to give. Essentials such as a travel ticket to go to and fro from home; one still is unable to buy. You notice that brother or sister is always walking and struggling. Even the countenance of their face is clouded, and peace of mind is far from them. By all means, we that have should be in a position to give and help.

For the poor will never cease from the land; therefore I command you, saying, 'You shall open your hand wide to your brother, to your poor and your needy, in your land.'

(**Deuteronomy 15:11**)

What the Bible Says About the Poor . . .

"Give to the one who asks you, and do not turn away from the one who wants to borrow from you" (**Matthew 5:42**) **NIV**. Jesus spoke these words when He went up on the mountainside and sat down teaching the multitudes. The idea behind this was to indicate how children of God should live and act towards people who are lacking. Jesus Christ Himself demonstrated the act of giving to us (the poor): *"The Spirit of the Lord is on me, because he has anointed me to preach good news to the poor"* (**Luke 4:18**) **NIV**.

We may have not been poor or needy physically, but before Christ reached out to us we were poor spiritually—knowing nothing of the kingdom of God.

John the Baptist (cousin of Jesus), who had been given the ministry to preach the remissions of sins, spoke to the people saying: *"The man with two tunics should share with him who has none, and the one who has food should do the same"* **(Luke 3:11) NIV**. Jesus Himself also spoke saying: *"Sell your possessions and give to the poor. Provide purses for yourselves that will not wear out, a treasure in heaven that will not be exhausted, where no thief comes near and no moth destroys"* **(Luke 12:33) NIV**.

Jesus by no means ever casted away the poor, but rather intended to meet their needs. For a Christian to practice this form of righteousness in truth, it automatically shows the kind of heart they have. The bible actually states when you lend to the poor you are actually lending to God and He will reward you back—*"He who has pity on the poor lends to the LORD, And He will pay back what he has given"* **(Proverbs 19:17)**.

Receiving Blessing When Considering the Poor . . .

Whenever we attempt to reflect on the poor to offer a helping hand, God will begin to act favorably in our lives. Below are five things the Lord has promise to all those who consider the poor. **Psalms 41:1-3**:

1) *"Blessed is he who considers the poor; The LORD will deliver him in time of trouble" (Verse 1)*—When troubles arrive, God will remember your care for the poor and release you from the hour of tribulation.

2) *"The LORD will preserve him and keep him alive" (Verse 2)*—Preserve meaning save, protect, safeguard. God will do all in His power to keep you alive.

3) *"And he will be blessed on the earth" (Verse 2)*—To be blessed is to be given the empowerment from God to achieve results others cannot achieve.

4) *"You will not deliver him to the will of his enemies" (Verse 2)*—Physical and spiritual enemies are constantly plotting and scheming, but as a result of caring for the poor the Lord will not deliver you into their will.

5) *"The LORD will strengthen him on his bed of illness" (Verse 3)*—The Lord will sustain you through illness.

Take a look at this powerful scripture.

At Caesarea there was a man named Cornelius, a centurion in what was known as the Italian Regiment. He and all his family were devout and God-fearing; he gave generously to those in need and prayed to God regularly. One day at about three in the afternoon he had a vision. He distinctly saw an angel of God, who came to him and said, "Cornelius!" Cornelius stared at him in fear. "What is it, Lord?" he asked. The angel answered, "Your prayers and gifts to the poor have come up as a memorial offering before God.

(Acts 10:1-4) NIV

In the book of Galatians, Apostles James, Peter and John recognized that God entrusted the gospel to Paul and Barnabas to preach to the Gentiles. After they agreed for Paul and Barnabas to preach to the Gentiles, the Apostles told them to keep doing what they were doing, which was to remember the poor. It was besides God had called them to do, but a key ingredient for them to do.

James, Peter and John, those reputed to be pillars, gave me and Barnabas the right hand of fellowship when they recognized the grace given to me. They agreed that we should go to the Gentiles, and they to the Jews. All they asked was that we should continue to remember the poor, the very thing I was eager to do.

(Galatians 2:9-10) NIV

Dangers of Ignoring the Poor . . .

If you knew a poor and needy person was in your mist and you had the ability to help, how would you act?

The bible teaches us to help one another. Giving to the poor (*in most cases*) should be seen as a long-term act rather than short-term act, to the extent where a positive change is made in the life of the needy. Remember, it's not just money; it could even be in a form of offering a helpless church member a lift after a church service. The idea is to physically help the person through their struggles by your giving.

Suppose a brother or sister is without clothes and daily food. If one of you says to him, "Go I wish you well; keep warm and well fed," but does nothing about his physical needs, what good is it?

(James 2:15-16) NIV

There was a rich man who was dressed in purple and fine linen and lived in luxury every day. At his gate was laid a beggar named Lazarus, covered with sores and longing to eat what fell from the rich man's table. Even the dogs came and licked his sores. The time came when the beggar died and the angels carried him to Abraham's side. The rich man also died and was buried. In hell, where he was in torment, he looked up and saw Abraham far away, with Lazarus by his side. So he called to him, 'Father Abraham, have pity on me and send Lazarus to dip the tip of his finger in water and cool my tongue, because I am in agony in this fire.'

(Luke 16:19-24) NIV

You realize that the rich man has been cast into a place where he is in great pain according to the bible, because he failed to help the poor. According to the Word of God the poor man only desired to eat the food that fell from the table (the scraps), but the rich man refused to give him that. Many of us pray and ask God for a breakthrough, when in actual fact we have dealt harshly with the poor— *"If a man shuts his ears to the cry of the poor, he too will cry out and not be answered"* **(Proverbs 21:13) NIV**.

In the book of Deuteronomy, Moses also revealed the danger of ignoring the poor among you: *"Beware lest there be a wicked thought in your heart, saying, 'The seventh year, the year of release, is at hand,' and your eye be evil against your poor brother and you give him nothing, and he cry out to the LORD against you, and it become sin among you"* **(Deuteronomy 15:9)**.

So far we have seen how God wants us to help those in need, and has also made us aware through scriptures, the dangers of ignoring the poor. King Nebuchadnezzar was at a point in his life where God was about to run him out of his kingdom for a season. But in an attempt to help him, Daniel advised him to be righteous and show mercy to the poor.

Therefore, O king, let my advice be acceptable to you; break off your sins by being righteous, and your iniquities by showing mercy to the poor. Perhaps there may be a lengthening of your prosperity."

(Daniel 4:27)

Looking to Jesus, the author and the finisher of our faith, how would Jesus act?

I remember a time where Jesus had been teaching the multitude for three days straight, and His concern was on their wellbeing. Refusing to send them away hungry, Jesus made it His business to meet their physical needs.

Now Jesus called His disciples to Himself and said," I have compassion on the multitude, because they have now continued with Me three days and have nothing to eat. And I do not want to send them away hungry, lest they faint on the way."

(Matthew 15:32)

Sometimes it's not just about our prayers for the needy that count. If this was the case, Jesus would have turned around and said *"I bless you with the spirit of sustainability not to faint."* But we see Jesus doing otherwise. His compassion led Him to gather His team and consider how best to meet their needs. In a similar circumstance in the book of Mark, His disciples told Jesus the day was far spent, therefore send the multitude away that they may buy food for themselves. But Jesus answered in the most perfect way by saying, *"You give them something to eat."* Thus implying they had a duty to provide.

When the day was now far spent, His disciples came to him and said "This is a deserted place, and already the hour is late. Send them away, that they may go into the surrounding country and villages and buy themselves bread; for they have nothing to eat." But He answered and said to them, "You give them something to eat."

(Mark 6:35-37)

In both affairs Jesus was moved with compassion and by no means left them dependent or vulnerable. Supposing He did and they fainted, how would that look on Jesus?

Jesus knew better so He did better, James will go on to write, *"Therefore, to him who knows to do good and does not do it, to him it is sin"* (**James 4:17**). Not only do we know that Jesus is without sin, Jesus is the word of God. So it was virtually impossible for Jesus to agree with the disciples and say, *"Multitude feed yourself!"*

God Himself is the perfect example to imitate. The bible reveals that God in fact feeds His people with food, both spiritual and physical food—*"The eyes of all look expectantly to You, and You give them their food in due season"* (**Psalms 145:15**).

My Testimony . . .

KNIGHTSBRIDGE

At times, before my wife and I were married, we use to go out and evangelize together. The Lord later touched our hearts to start feeding the poor in the process. On one occasion, the Lord led us to Knightsbridge in London (one of the most renowned sites in the United Kingdom which is considered a place of wealth and fortune). I remember glancing at watches for sale at a particular store with prices ranging from £20k to £250k.

There we discovered a few people that were homeless, some drunkards, others crippled, all begging for spare change as shoppers pass by. Most were located outside the stores on the high street, while others were in the parks nearby. We prayed and prophesied as the Spirit of God gave us utterance to the ones we found.

I remember speaking to one particular guy who sat on the floor under a shop shelter. We offered him food as we did the others, but to our surprise this man refused. I marveled within me as to why he would do this? He then started to grumble and position himself away from us still refusing to eat. Then suddenly the Lord opened my eyes and I began to speak to him of his own child hood; how he yearns to be an actor, but somehow the enemy re-arranged his destiny and caused him to amount to nothing. Turning hastily to the sound of my voice, he began to open up and to speak of his dreams and ambitions of becoming an actor. He also had a celebrity magazine in his hand that he was reading. He explained how he likes to read about their lifestyle as it inspires him to keep dreaming. At this point I began telling him about the love of Jesus. Tears rolled down his face as I began ministering the Word of God to him. After accepting the food he had refused earlier, we prayed with him and departed.

BURGER KING

The night was dark and cold. It was the beginning of the year 2011 when my wife and I came across an Asian man who sluggishly swept himself across the car park of Burger King begging for help. Upon spotting us, he began to follow shouting—*"Sir, please, I don't want money—I just want your blessings"*. After giving him my attention he spoke and informed me how he had lost everything from his profession to his wife and children, and many more.

I responded by asking him *"what do you want me to do for you?"* (Having just seen two other young guys walk straight passed him). He spoke and said with an indistinct voice, *"sir all I want is your blessings"*. I began preaching the good news of Jesus Christ to him. Although he had a different religion, He wanted to know more about this Jesus. Afterwards, we prayed with him as he prayed the sinner's prayer, confessing his sins to Christ, and denouncing his other gods.

My wife being with child stood overseeing everything. She then urged me to buy him something to eat from Burger King as the night was dark and cold. I had just bought this jacket from Next that I had only worn three times, but I felt compelled to take it off and give it to him as a token of the love of Jesus. I started to undo the buttons as the man stood by embracing his meal to his chest, and I said to him *"Sir I love you and this is the love of Jesus, take this and stay warm"*. He began to smile, taking hold of the coat saying *"Thank you"* and we departed.

CHAPTER 3

Understanding Worship

Israel, what does the Lord your God want you to do? He wants you to fear Him, follow all His directions, love Him, and worship Him with all your heart and with all your soul.
Deuteronomy 10:12 (God's Word Translation)

Religious worship is a well known practice performed in nearly every corner of the world by various individuals, societies and groups.

Worship can be seen as one of the most sacred attributes for instigating a divine connection between a Supreme Being and man. From a Christian's perspective, to worship is to live the holy life that is acceptable and pleasing unto God—"*I appeal to you therefore, brothers, by the mercies of God, to present your bodies as a living sacrifice, holy and acceptable to God, which is your spiritual worship*"

(Romans 12:1) ESV.

Many Christians today are yet to grasp the full understanding of God's expectations from us in worship. It is always beneficial when you *'fully understand'* what is expected of you, verses *'merely understanding'* what's required of you. When we have the full knowledge and understanding of anything we do, we are able to do it better. No wonder the bible instructs us saying, "*In all thy getting, get understanding*" **(Proverbs 4:7)**. Understanding is the key to everything.

In The Beginning . . .

In the beginning when the Lord began to move and have fellowship with His people, (just when the laws were introduced), He commanded them through Moses to have no other god before Him, nor to serve nor worship them.

And God spoke all these words, saying: "I am the LORD your God, who brought you out of the land of Egypt, out of the house of bondage. "You shall have no other gods before Me. "You shall not make for yourself a carved image—any likeness of anything that is in heaven above, or that is in the earth beneath, or that is in the water under the earth; you shall not bow down o them nor serve them.

(Exodus 20:1-5)

As time moved on, in the book of Deuteronomy, Moses preaches and reinstates the Laws of God to the ones who were chosen to posses the promise land. Moses explained that upon entering the land, the manner of which the Lord should be worshiped. They were prescribed a place of worship selected from God to have His name there for His dwelling. In doing this, God's people will be ordered to attend and serve Him there.

You shall not worship the LORD your God with such things. "But you shall seek the place where the LORD your God chooses, out of all your tribes, to put His name for His dwelling place; and there you shall go. There you shall take your burnt offerings, your sacrifices, your tithes, the heave offerings of your hand, your vowed offerings, your freewill offerings, and the firstborn of your herds and flocks.

(Deuteronomy 12:4-6)

Shiloh was an ancient city; its connection to the bible was held at one point as an assembly place for the children of Israel for various meetings. A time came when Shiloh became a centre point of worship for the Israelites—*"Year after year this man went up from his town to worship and sacrifice to the LORD Almighty at Shiloh"* **(1 Samuel 1:3) NIV**.

Abram, a man called by God, received a command from the Lord in **Genesis 12** to leave his land. It is believed that Abram lived in the land called Ur, a place where the people worshiped many gods. Ur, for instance was the site of a great ziggurat or temple tower dedicated to the Sumerian moon-god, Nanna. Other temples at Ur honored An, Enlil, Enki and Nin-gal. Theologians believe Abram was said to have worshiped and served them before being called by God.

God made a covenant with His people telling them *"If you will indeed obey My voice and keep my covenant, then you shall be a special treasure to Me above all people"* **(Exodus 19:5)**. However, at times God usually ended up handing them over to be afflicted by their enemies because of the evil they committed.

Once again the Israelites sinned against the Lord by worshipping the Baals and the Astartes, as well as the gods of Syria, of Sidon, of Moab, of Ammon, and of Philistia. They abandoned the Lord and stopped worshiping him. So the Lord became angry with the Israelites, and let the Philistines and the Ammonites conquer them.

(Judges 10:6-7) GNT

Each time God delivered His people to be subdued by the enemy, they were not free to serve and worship God in accordance to His commands. During these times, God still operated under the first covenant which involved animal sacrifices and burnt offerings. The question I asked myself—Was this what God wanted for His people? And if so, how would they still be able to facilitate these requirements, having being placed under severe bondage and slavery by neighboring tribes?

When God's children where in slavery, God revealed to Moses that He had heard the cries of His people and choose Moses to lead them out of Egypt. Moses obeying the voice of God, returned to Egypt and pleaded with Pharaoh saying, *"Please, let us go three days' journey into the desert and sacrifice to the LORD our God, lest He fall upon us with pestilence or with the sword"* **(Exodus 5:3)**.

A time came when there was a battle, and the enemies who survived in a war against Israel, were commanded to worship the Lord.

Then all the survivors from the nations that have attacked Jerusalem will go there each year to worship the Lord Almighty as king and to celebrate the Festival of Shelters. If any nation refuses to go and worship the Lord Almighty as king, then rain will not fall on their land. If the Egyptians refuse to celebrate the Festival of Shelters, then they will be struck by the same disease that the Lord will send on every nation that refuses to go. This will be the punishment that will fall on Egypt and on all the other nations if they do not celebrate the Festival of Shelters.

(Zechariah 14:16-19) GNT

In **Numbers 28 and 29**, Moses also taught the people a range of offerings God required from them, which is a form of worship. These offerings were:

- Daily
- Sabbath
- Monthly
- Passover
- Feast of Weeks
- Feast of Trumpets
- Day of Atonement
- Feast of Tabernacles

How could these offerings be kept if the people were to be taken captive? Would this mean God's children would go throughout a period of not worshiping Him in accordance to the law?

There were other suggestions in the bible which indicated why and how the children of God ended up in captivity. But by God's love, we come to see the Lord sending a deliverer to rescue His people. God always had a plan to deliver His people once they call to Him. But what happens when the Lord sentence His people to forty, seventy, or even four hundred years in bondage? After reasoning with myself, I came to the conclusion that only the true worshipers of God will be able to stand.

I remember the days of Daniel and his three friends when they were in captivity.

In the third year of the reign of Jehoiakim King of Judah, Nebuchadnezzar king of Babylon came to Jerusalem and besieged it. And the Lord gave Jehoiakim king of Judah into his hand, with some of the articles of the house of God, which he carried into the land of Shinar to the house of his god; and he brought the articles into the treasure house of his god.

(Daniel 1:1-2)

One day in the Babylonian palace, King Nebuchadnezzar passed a decree that the newly built image of gold should be worshipped by all men in the palace. Now Daniel's three friends being upright, righteous and lovers of God refused this thing. **(See Daniel 3:8-18)**.

Later on in the chapter, we see that God saved Shadrach, Meshach and Abed—Nego from the punishment that was said to come from disobeying the Kings request.

But my only question in this matter was what happened to the other Jews that were held in the palace amongst the three boys that refused to worship the image? Or were there only four people that were taken captive by king Nebuchadnezzar? Certainly not, the bible says in Daniel 3:18 there were certain Jews who disregarded the king's command. This clearly means there were other Jews who obeyed the king's command and worshipped the golden image.

Shadrach, Meshach and Abed—Nego are what I would call *'true worshippers'* of God.

Shadrach, Meshach and Abed—Nego answered and said to the king, "O Nebuchadnezzar, we have no need to answer you in this matter. "If that is the case, our God whom we serve is able to deliver us from the burning fiery furnace, and He will deliver us from your hand O king. But if not, let it be known to you, O King that we do not serve your gods, nor will we worship the gold image which you have set up.

(Daniel 3:16-18)

They trembled at God's word and served Him fully. A price the other Jews were not willing to pay. The three boys could have easily worshiped the image like others and asked God for forgiveness later, but they fully understood the concept of worship. Obedience to God's word can also be seen as a form of worship.

In the New King James Bible (NKJV), Isaiah 66 starts with sub-heading **'True Worship and False'**. Verse 1-4 speaks of two sets of people, one who tremble's at the word of God (*True Worshipers*) and the other who chooses their own ways (*False Worshipers*). We will examine this in more details.

True and False Worship . . .

The very nature of most human beings is that they feel compelled to worshiping someone or something. In one instance, God spoke to Moses concerning the sky and the galaxy. *"And take heed, lest you lift your eyes to heaven, and when you see the sun, the moon, and the stars, all the host of heaven, you feel driven to worship them and serve them, which the LORD your God has given to all the people under the whole heaven as a heritage"* **(Deuteronomy 4:19)**.

In having many religions and beliefs, many people around the world have become separated and alienated from the one true God, the Creator and the Possessor of heaven and earth. Through this deception, many have come to worship the creation rather than the Creator.— *"They exchanged the truth of God for a lie, and worshiped and served created things rather than the Creator—who is forever praised"* **(Romans 1:25) NIV**.

During my lunch breaks at work, I'm very mindful of meeting new people in an attempt to share Jesus with someone. For this reason, I always keep a smile and a friendly approach on my face. In doing this, I began developing friendships with various people; one being a young Asian man who works in a local news agent. On one occasion, I met and spoke with his elderly uncle who often came by the news agent to visit. This man appeared to be one of the wisest men I've ever met. He spoke very plain but very insightful with words that accompanied wise proverbs. At first, I stood amazed and concluded it to be down to his old age wisdom mixed with life experiences that gave him such a cutting edge. On another day, he revealed to me in a conversation his religion and who he worshiped. He said in his religion they worship the five elements that are vital to life, as without them, life will be impossible to live—*Fire, Water, Earth, Air and Wind.* I marveled vigorously, the first bible page I saw when I closed my eyes was the book of **Romans 1:18**.

For the wrath of God is revealed from heaven against all ungodliness and unrighteousness of men, who suppress the truth in unrighteousness, because what may be known of God is manifest in them, for God has shown it to them. For since the creation of the world His invisible attributes are clearly seen, being understood by the things that are made, even His eternal power and Godhead, so that they are without excuse, because, although they knew God, they did not glorify Him as God, nor were thankful, but became futile in their thoughts, and their foolish hearts were darkened. Professing to be wise, they become fools, and changed the glory of the incorruptible God into an image made like corruptible man and birds and four-footed animals and creeping things.

(Romans 1:18-23)

Many religions claim to worship the one true God, which can be administrated in various ways depending on the religion and belief of the person. Often, many religions are perplexed on the Christian belief as to how Jesus the Son of man can be worshiped? Some laugh and ridicule the whole matter, asking *'How can a man be worshipped?'* But what they don't know is worshipping God through Jesus Is the only gateway to Heaven.

At the birth of Jesus, Matthew records wise men travelling from the East to Jerusalem to worship baby Jesus.

Now after Jesus was born in Bethlehem of Judea in the days of Herod the king, behold, wise men from the East came to Jerusalem, saying, "Where is He who has been born King of the Jews? For we have seen His star in the East and have come to worship Him."

(Matthew 2:1-2)

God has placed all things under His Son's authority, which includes Christ being worshipped.—*"Has in these last days spoken to us by His Son, whom He has appointed heir of all things, through whom also He made the worlds"* **(Hebrews 1:2).** Verse 6 tells us that Angels worship the Son of God—*"Let all the angels of God worship Him"* **(Hebrews 1:6)**. Even with this status, Jesus came in the form of men though He was equal to God.

Who, being in the form of God, did not consider it robbery to be equal with God, but made Himself of no reputation, taking the form of a bondservant, and coming in the likeness of men.

(Philippians 2:6-7)

We learn from scriptures that even unclean spirits recognize Jesus as the Son of God. The book of Mark gives an account of a man who was possessed by an unclean spirit and dwelt among the tombs. Upon seeing Jesus, he ran and worshiped Him, pleading with the Lord not to torment him; for the unclean spirit recognized the power and authority Jesus had.

When he saw Jesus from afar, he ran and worshipped Him. And he cried out with a loud voice and said, "What have I to do with You, Jesus, Son of the Most High God? I implore You by God that You do not torment me.

(Mark 5:6-7)

This type of worship was a sign that Jesus is the head of all things. The bible says, "And *you are complete in Him, who is the head of all principality and power*" **(Colossians 2:10)**. So we know that the demons are subjected to His authority. The bible foretells us that a time will come, and in fact is already here, that we shall all stand before the judgment seat of Christ and confess *"As I live, says the Lord, Every knee shall bow to Me, And every tongue shall confess to God"* **(Romans 14:11)**.

If men choose to bypass the Son of God and offer direct worship to God, such a person is not abiding under God's commands; neither can they truly be worshipping the Lord God of Israel. Jesus Himself said in the book of John, *"I am the way, the truth, and the life. No one comes to the Father except through Me"* **(John 14:6).**

Back in the days growing up I use to hear people say *"it's all the same God but just in a different form"*. But the statement that Jesus made in **John 14:6**, enabled me to brush such believes far from me.

The Disciples of Jesus were once travelling on a boat that was tossed by the waves; for the wind was contrary to their journey. Whilst this was happening, Jesus was not present with them, but later showed up walking on the sea intended to pass them by, stopped and entered the boat causing the wind to cease. His disciples were astonished when they saw the wind obeying him, and all they could do is worship Him—*"Then those who were in the boat came and worshipped Him, saying, "Truly You are the Son of God"* **(Matthew 14:33)**.

Importance of Worship . . .

Worship is not only powerful but important. It gives us access to the divine nature of God, where you can experience His awesome presence, power, healing, blessings etc. For instance, most of us (if not all of us), have seen people in church with some form of sickness or illness, but during praise and worship, they received their healing, others through serving the Lord faithfully, or simply obeying God's word which are all a form of worship.

Worship the LORD your God, and his blessing will be on your food and water. I will take away sickness from among you.

(Exodus 23:25) NIV

Certain countries (with other religions besides Christianity), view worship as an important practice. One religion has bells and alarms placed in the heart of the city which sounds off at various times, to serve as a calling for a national worship. These groups of people could be in the middle of a transaction or something twice as important, but each time the bell sounds off, people would run collectively to gather before their god to pray and worship.

I once questioned God in my heart asking, *"When You look down from Your holy hill, how do You feel when You see these non Christians worshipping their gods in total diligence and understanding?"*

Satan knows the importance of worship and tried to tempt Jesus into worshipping him.

And the devil said to Him, "All this authority I will give You, and their glory; for this has been delivered to me, and I give it to whomever I wish. "Therefore, if You will worship before me, all will be Yours.

(Luke 4:6-7)

Jesus replied saying . . .

Get behind Me Satan! For it is written, 'You shall worship the LORD your God, and Him only you shall serve.

(Luke 4:8)

But of course this will not stop Satan; he is still after Gods Worship. He looks to mislead God's people through deception, that they may render to him worship in order for him to take full control claiming them. By doing this, the devil lies in great expectation to receive his harvest of rejected souls at the end of time. According to the book of Revelations, he fully understands that the names that are not written in the book of Life will be reserved for him. So if he can manage to deceive God's elect, how happy he will be?

All who dwell on the earth will worship him, whose names have not been written in the Book of Life of the Lamb slain from the foundations of the world.

(Revelation 13:8)

When you understand worship, you will begin to be enlightened on how blessed mankind is to be chosen by God to be part-takers of worshiping Him. God could have easily reserved the act of worship exclusively for angels; but rather, choose to involve us in this wonderful calling. After all, if we don't worship God, it's not like He won't be worshiped. The bible tells us in Revelations that the living creatures and the twenty four elders constantly worship Him in heaven.

Whenever the living creatures give glory and honor and thanks to Him who sits on the throne, who lives forever and ever, the twenty-four elders fall down before Him who sits on the throne and worship Him who lives forever and ever, and cast their crowns before the throne, saying, "You are worthy, O Lord, To receive glory and honor and power; For You created all things, And by Your will they exist and were created.

(Revelation 4:9-11)

There was a certain woman in the bible called Lydia, who was described as a seller of purple goods and a worshiper of the Lord. Her relationship with God (*being a worshiper*), allowed the keys of Heaven to be dropped in her hands. God choose her out of the other women to comprehend the scriptures that were being preached by the Apostles. At the end of their meeting, God had given her favor and the opportunity to invite the Apostles as guests into her home.

Now a certain women named Lydia heard us. She was a seller of purple from the city of Thyatira, who worshiped God. The Lord opened her heart to heed the things spoken by Paul. And when she and her household were baptized, she begged us, saying, "If you have judged me to be faithful to the Lord, come to my house and stay." So she persuaded us.

(Acts 16:14-15)

You can just imagine the type of further teachings and blessings she received the time the Apostles spent at her home. Her connection came through being a worshiper. The bible says the Lord opened her heart to heed the things spoken by Apostle Paul. As children of the Most High God, we ought to place worship at the pinnacle of our heart since God requires this from us—*"You shall worship the LORD your God, and Him only you shall serve"* (**Luke 4:8**).

Today . . .

The understanding of Worship in the bible is largely extensive, but the essential concept in scripture is *'service'*. Looking at our lives today, we know the way we are called to serve and worship God is different from the days of old—*In some aspects.*

God once accepted specific burnt offerings and sacrifices as a form of worship from His people. Even at the Christening of baby Jesus (being Mary's first born), animal sacrifices were made in accordance to God's law—*"Every male who opens the womb shall be called holy to the Lord")* and *to offer a sacrifice according to what is said in the law of the Lord, "A pair of turtledoves or two young pigeons"* (**Luke 2:23-24**). Up until the death of Jesus, these laws were still in operation, until He became the last and final physical sacrifice made to God—*"By that will we have been sanctified through the offering of the body of Jesus Christ once for all"* (**Hebrews 10:10**).

Understanding how God was worshiped then, as well as knowing how we ought to worship God now, is very fundamental. This is the beginning of *'Understanding Worship'*. Knowing this, we can find various examples in the bible of people who pleased God and others who displeased Him through their worship. Others where necessary, avoided reliving the mistakes of those who provoked the Lord to anger.

While Israel was staying in Shittim, the men began to indulge in sexual immorality with Moabite women, who invited them to the sacrifices to their gods. The people ate and bowed down before these gods. So Israel joined in worshipping the Baal of Peor. And the Lord's anger burned against them.

(Numbers 25:1-3) NIV

The key for us today is found in John's gospel. Jesus asked a Samaritan woman for a drink. She was surprised that Jesus spoke to her; for the Jews were said to have no dealings with Samaritans. Jesus began to reveal personal issues about the woman that had been the truth as well as a mystery to her. The woman was amazed and referred to Him as a *'Prophet'*, because she bore witness to His statement. Carrying on with their conversation, the topic of Worship came up and Jesus revealed how the Father now requires His worship.

The woman said to Him, "Sir, I perceive that You are a prophet. "Our fathers worshipped on this mountain, and you Jews say that in Jerusalem is the place where one ought to worship." Jesus said to her, "Woman, believe Me, the hour is coming when you will neither on this mountain, nor in Jerusalem, worship the Father. "You worship what you do not know; we know what we worship, for salvation is of the Jews. "But the hour is coming, and now is, when the true worshipers will worship the Father in spirit and in truth; for the Father is seeking such to worship Him. "God is Spirit, and those who worship Him must worship in spirit and truth.

(John 4:19-24)

The Act of Worshiping in Spirit . . .

Worship is not limited to just praising and singing hymns, but bringing our whole being under the total submission of God. Apostle Paul said "*For God is my witness whom I serve with my spirit in the gospel of His son*" **(Romans 1:9) The Gideons International.**

I appeal to you therefore, brothers, by the mercies of God, to present your bodies as a living sacrifice, holy and acceptable to God, which is your spiritual worship.

(Romans 12:1) ESV

In order for us to offer spiritual worship we must first be in the spirit; walking by faith not by sight.

When we look at the story of Cain and Abel, the bible tells us in Genesis that a time came when the two boys brought an offering to God. Now their offerings were a sign of who they served. They worshiped God by presenting an offering. We read and find out that God respected one and despised the other. Why was this?

It is not only down to what they offered, but I believe there were some significance in how they offered their offering. The bible clearly indicates that Abel brought the firstborn of his offering, whilst Cain brought an offering of the fruit of the ground. This could be interpreted that Cain failed to bring the first fruit to God (the portion God requires), and therefore settled for any random part as an offering for God. But it also comes down to the understanding of worship, which I believe God wants us to have just like Abel had.

Abel was more of a '*man of God*' than his brother. He was able to offer what was right, which lead to him and his offering being accepted. It also means, Abel must have lived a life, or had times where he was in fellowship with God, to be able to know what God required.

27

By faith Abel offered to God a more excellent sacrifice than Cain, through which he obtained witness that he was righteous, God testifying of his gifts; and through it he being dead still speaks.

(Hebrews 11:4)

Now Cain, in my opinion is more of a flesh man rather than a faith man. The bible says, *"And in the process of time it came to pass that Cain brought an offering of the fruit of ground to the LORD"* **(Genesis 4:3).** But later we find out that the fruit of the ground that he offered, God did not accept. Notice how God holds you and your offering together. **Genesis 4:5** says, *"but He did not respect Cain and his offering"*. God denied Cain's offering because, in the sight of God, Cain did not do what was right—*"If you do well, will you not be accepted?"* **(Genesis 4:7).**

Now the question is how will Cain or anybody know how to do well? The answer is simple—by seeking the One who approves. The bible teaches us that this is our responsibility—*"For the fruit of the Spirit is in all goodness, righteousness, and truth finding out what is acceptable to the Lord"* **(Ephesians 5:9-10).**

The book of Hebrews tells us Abel's faith allowed him to offer a better sacrifice than Cain. Therefore, one may question the authenticity of Cain's faith, as the bible clearly states—*"Without faith it is impossible to please God"* **(Hebrews 11:6) NIV**. If Cain had faith and walked with God, then perhaps he could have offered God a better sacrifice that would have been accepted. But the fact remains, Cain was missing this vital ingredient in his life so even before he presented his offering to God, it was already refused. From this, we learnt how Cain became angry then later rose against his brother and killed him.

Since we are children of the light, it is imperative we check what's on the inside of us—*"Examine yourselves to see if you are in the faith"* **(2 Corinthians 13:5) NIV**. For instance, bitterness may be dwelling on the inside of us, and instead of dealing with it, we act like it's not there, pushing it aside whilst worshiping God. The bible says in **Hebrews 12:15,** *"Looking carefully lest anyone fall short of the grace of God; lest any root of bitterness springing up cause trouble, and by this many become defiled"*. Can God accept such things living on the inside of us when He has called us to be holy? Certainly not! Because it is written, *"Be holy, for I am holy"*.

Even if your brother has something against you, the bible teaches us to reconcile with them first before offering our gifts/offerings at the altar.

Therefore, if you are offering your gift at the altar and there remember that your brother has something against you, leave your gift there in front of the altar. First go and be reconciled to your brother; then come and offer your gift.

(Matthew 5:23-24) NIV

The Act of Worshiping in Truth . . .

Offering God a physical act of worship can be seen as a bold outward expression of who you serve.

At age 16 (during college years), one day I felt the Lord nudge me saying *"Justin come up and worship Me, every morning, evening and night"*. I smiled as I began to feel His peace. One morning, I remember being woken up for the first time by His touch. I crawled to my window ledge on my knees looking out of the window, glancing at the sky. I had never seen such striking colors before. I remember the sky being purple with a touch of pink, mix with a lighter blue and a seal of yellow. I was full of tears but I was so happy. I had no idea what I was going to say or do in my hour of worship, but to my surprise I reached for my bible and landed on the page where Daniel prayed having his window opened towards Jerusalem, kneeling down giving thanks to God three times a day. I knew that God was nearer to me than I thought. This is a custom I began to do up onto this very day, thanking Him with my windows opened.

To add to this, I stumbled on **Psalms 5** which I use as morning devotion, **Psalms 141** as evening devotion and **Psalms 134** as devotion for night. It reminds me of Anna the prophetess in the bible, although people may have known her for this, she took this very seriously. It said that she worshiped God in the temple, every day and night with fasting.

There was also a prophetess, Anna, the daughter of Phanuel, of the tribe of Asher. She was very old; she had lived with her husband seven years after her marriage, and then she was a widow until she was eighty four. She never left the temple but worshipped night and day fasting and praying.

(Luke 2:36-37) NIV

It's Not Where You Are It's Where You Are From . . .

God, the Creator of mankind, made us who we are for His purpose. Throughout the study of history, we have come to know that there are around 196 countries in the world, each bearing its own unique language, or some bearing similarities with others.

Most countries like Africa are made up of groups of people from various tribes and sects, each having different traditions and customs. Customs meaning a set of guidelines that's been in operation for over hundreds of decades; possibly installed by ancestors, which are then taught and passed down to the next generation to abide by. Tradition which is similar in nature but is defined as a ritual or belief handed down within a society, still maintained in the present, with origins dated from the past. Customs and traditions we inherit from our country can be very good, especially when introduced to a person's life from birth. Normally, it should provide good morals for one to adhere by. Growing up, my mother taught us the custom of praying every night before sleeping, now that I am a young man I keep this practice which she had taught back then.

Having said this, when we give our live to Christ, practices which are outside the faith should be carefully considered, as some traditions and customs clandestinely teaches people to serve, even worship ancestors, and foreign gods, rather than the God of Abraham. At first it can be very subtle because in your mind your still serving and worshiping God. But when you zoom in a little closely you see these things can actually become a snare to you.

They worshiped the LORD, but they also served their own gods in accordance with the customs of the nations from which they had been brought.

(2 Kings 17:33) NIV

I have some Christian friends from Ghana, who are all firm believers in Christ; however they are also strong and devout to their tribal traditions. Being from a royal tribe like me, one of their practices (at that time) required a new person to sit on their family home throne where they would attend village meetings and discuss family issues. But in these meetings they explained certain people will be called to attend, including witch doctors. I explained it would have been better for you to take yourself out of the equation and focus more on Christ.

Then the Pharisees and some of the scribes came together to Him, having come from Jerusalem. Now when they saw some of His disciples eat bread with defiled, that is, with unwashed hands, they found fault. For the Pharisees and all the Jews do not eat unless they wash their hands in a special way, holding the tradition of the elders. When they come from the marketplace, they do not eat unless they wash. And there are many other things which they have received and hold, like the washing of cups, pitchers, copper vessels, and couches. Then the Pharisees and scribes asked Him, "Why do Your disciples not walk according to the tradition of the elders, but eat bread with unwashed hands?" He answered and said "Well did Isaiah prophesy of you hypocrites, as it is written; "This people honors Me with their lips, But their heart is far from Me. And in vain they worship Me, Teaching as doctrines the commandments of men." For laying aside the commandments of God you hold the tradition of men—the washing of pitchers and cups, and many other such things you do." He said to them "All too well you reject the commandments of God, that you may keep your tradition. For Moses said "Honor your father and your mother, and He who curses father or mother, let him be put to death, But you say "If a man says to his father or mother, "Whatever profit you might have received from me is Corban"—(that is, a gift to God) then you no longer let him do anything for his father or mother, making the word of God of no effect through your tradition which you have handed down. And many such things you do.

(Mark 7:1-13)

The time approached for God's people to journey to Jerusalem for the Feast of the Passover which was held every year. The Passover was said to commemorate the liberation of the Israelites from slavery in Egypt **(See Numbers 9 for further reading)**.

Jesus was a Jew, so there were times when He would take part in Jewish traditions. On one occasion, the bible recalls Joseph and Mary journeying to Jerusalem to attend the Passover with Jesus. Having performed all things according to the law of the Lord, they returned home. After journeying a day's journey, to their surprise they discovered Jesus was absent. This caused them to become terrified and sought for Him high and low, only to find Him back in Jerusalem teaching in the temple.

Why was this?

Even though Jesus obeyed the customs and laws of God's commands stated in Numbers 9, He was also very much interested in fulfilling His assignment which He described as *"My Father's business"* (**Luke 2:49**).

Being from (or born to) a particular country, there are certain customs and traditions we inherit knowingly or unknowingly from parents and/or forefathers. As stated earlier, these customs and traditions are set guidelines enforced throughout generations to generations. However, before embracing this, it is advisable to study and check the history behind these mores. After all, as born again Christians, we are now born out of our earthly family and into the family of God.

I remember one day (before me and my wife were married), a week before the Easter period, we were hanging out at her mums place when she told me, *"We need to buy fish for Good Friday"*, I replied, *"What for?"* . . . She then explained how it's a well known practice in Jamaica not to eat meat on Good Friday in honor of Jesus death. So I asked her to show me this in the bible and she replied, *"I don't know"*.

This is just one example of things we are taught growing up, having no understanding of, yet finding ourselves faithfully serving and adhering to. Although this may not appear to be harmful, the question one will need to ask themselves before embracing this is, *'who instructed it and was that person a believer?'* or better yet, did it come from Jesus?

Beware lest anyone cheat you through philosophy and empty deceit, according to the tradition of men, according to the basic principles of the world, and not according to Christ.

(Colossians 2:8)

When Apostle Paul addressed a similar topic, he made it very clear by saying the reality is in Christ.

Therefore do not let anyone judge you by what you eat or drink, or with regard to a religious festival, a New moon celebration or a Sabbath day. These are a shadow of the things that were to come; the reality, however is found in Christ.

(Colossians 2:16-17) NIV

It is very good we teach our children the heritage of our country. After all, they need to know where they are coming from if indeed they are from there. But let us do it with the spirit of God. Apostle Paul in the book of Colossians spoke of the freedom we have from human regulations through life with Christ.

These are all destined to perish with use, because they are based on human commands and teachings. Such regulations indeed have an appearance of wisdom, with their self-imposed worship, their false humility and their harsh treatment of the body, but they lack any value in restraining sensual indulgence.

(Colossians 2:22-23) NIV

A time came when Apostle Paul was ministering in Corinth. But the people could not receive the message that was given to him from the Lord, due to them holding firm to their own custom and traditions.

Now the Lord spoke to Paul in the night by a vision, "Do not be afraid, but speak and do not keep silent; for I am with you, and no one will attack you to hurt you; for I have many people in this city" And he continued there a year and six months, teaching the Word of God among them. When Gallio was proconsul of Achaia, the Jews with one accord rose up against Paul and brought him to the judgment seat, saying, "This fellow persuades men to worship God contrary to the Law".

(Acts 18:9-13)

I do not teach men to abandon their customs and traditions; after all this is where God has found it fit for us to be born in. But it does seem wise to me to instruct you to check and see if it's in line with the scriptures. The bible says the people in Berea were more fair-minded than the Thessalonica. Why? Because they searched the scriptures to find out if what Apostle Paul was teaching was true— *"These were more fair –minded than those in Thessalonica, in that they received the Word with all readiness, and searched the Scriptures daily to find out whether these things were so"* **(Acts 17:11)**.

Apostle Paul spoke saying, *"Imitate me, just as I also imitate Christ"* **(1 Corinthians 11:1)**. Apostle Paul, having so much to boast about such as his country, his background, and all his credentials, ended up saying Christ is all, and what he has received from birth he considers rubbish that he may embrace all of God's fullness.

Finally, my brethren, rejoice in the Lord. For me to write the same things to you is not tedious, but for you it is safe. Beware of dogs, beware of evil workers, beware of the mutilation! For we are the circumcision, who worship God in Spirit, rejoice in Christ Jesus, and have no confidence in the flesh, though I also might have confidence in the flesh. If anyone thinks he may have confidence in the flesh, I more so: circumcised the eighth day, of the stock of Israel, of the tribe of Benjamin, a Hebrew of the Hebrews; concerning the law, a Pharisee; concerning zeal, persecuting the church; concerning the righteousness which is in the law, blameless. But what things were gain to me, these I have counted loss for Christ. Yet indeed I also count all things loss for the excellence of the knowledge of Christ Jesus my Lord, for whom I have suffered the loss of all things, and count as rubbish, that I may gain Christ and be found in Him, not having my own righteousness, which is from the law, but that which is through faith in Christ, the righteousness which is from God by faith; that I may know Him and the power of His resurrection, and the fellowship of His sufferings, being conformed to His death, if, by any means, I may attain to the resurrection from the dead.

(Philippians 3:1-11)

Not all, but some traditional practices have an evil base from the onset. I remember when my nephew and niece where born, their grandparents who are Christians had a tradition from back home were newborns were to be offered or shown to the family gods, by lifting them up to the sky early in the morning within the first few days of their birth. My sister refused to allow this to happen. A few days later the Lord opened a terrific door for me, where I ended up passing through to say hello and she asked me to watch the children as she quickly ran down the road.

I agreed and had the opportunity to thank God Almighty for the gift of life and dedicated the babies through prayer by faith to the Lord.

Do not be unequally yoked together with unbelievers. For what fellowship has righteousness with lawlessness? And what communion has light with darkness? And what accord has Christ with Belial? Or what part has a believer with an unbeliever? And what agreement has the temple of God with Idols? For you are the temple of the living God. As God has said: I will dwell in them And walk among them. I will be their God, And they shall be My people" Therefore, Come out from among them And be separate, says the Lord. Do not touch what is unclean, And I will receive you" I will be a Father to you, And you shall be My sons and daughters, Says the LORD Almighty".

(2 Corinthians 6:14-17)

The Lord has called us to be holy so when we as Christians claim to be followers of Christ carrying out such practices, it rather angers the Lord and can also pollute our flesh and spirit —*"Therefore, having these promises, beloved, let us cleanse ourselves from all filthiness of the flesh and spirit, perfecting holiness in the fear of God"* **(2 Corinthians 7:1)**.

Let us therefore become a people of God having the very same mind that was found in Christ. Jesus was also aware of traditions, but at the end of the Passover meeting, Jesus began to do what He was called to do—*to Minister.*

Paul said *"For our citizenship is in heaven, from which we also eagerly wait for the Savior, the Lord Jesus Christ"* **(Philippians 3:20)**.

People of old had a mind set of being Heavenly Citizens by faith rather than of their own countries.

These all died in faith, not having received the promises, but having seen them afar off were assured of them, embraced them and confessed that they were strangers and pilgrims on the earth. For those who say such things declare plainly that they seek a homeland. And truly if they had called to mind that country from which they had come out, they would have had opportunity to return. But now they desire a better, that is, a heavenly county. Therefore God is not ashamed to be called their God, for He has prepared a city for them.

(Hebrews 11:13-16)

After all, the reason we are living is mainly to learn how to serve Him and worship Him here on earth, in order to prepare ourselves for the life to come with Him in eternity.

And there shall be no more curse, but the throne of God and of the Lamb shall be in it, and His servants shall serve Him.

(Revelation 22:3)

In conclusion, let us not be too much concerned with our countries tradition and beliefs, but rather with God's word. In being too concern, you may miss out in God's way, embracing another.

Testimony . . .

On March 4ᵗʰ 2008, I was dismissed from a job I had in a college. The basis of my dismissal was for not completing the probation period. It placed me in a tight situation being 23 years old with no job. I had graduated from Greenwich University two years prior to this with a BA (Hons) Business degree. I struggled for months, going without money; I drove a new type Astra 2006 sports 1.9 model coupe. How was I going to maintain this? How was I going to eat?

I applied for countless jobs and heard nothing. I prayed and cried again and again, still nothing. Four months had come and gone and those four months felt like 4 years. In July 2008, a still voice travelled swiftly through the openings of the air, I gazed and marveled as I heard the voice say, *"If you are seeking work, worship me now"*. I fell prostrated and started worshiping the Lord, for I knew it was Him that had spoken.

A few days later at church my pastor had an anointing service where he gave a word to the entire congregation. When my time arrived after queuing up, my pastor (being under the influence of the Holy Spirit), laid his hands on my head and said, *"If you seek Me in this time of unemployment, I will perform a miracle in your life. I the Lord have called you into ministry"*.

On Monday 14ᵗʰ July 2008, I began working in a Law firm.

CHAPTER 4

The Blessing

And of Naphtali he said, O Naphtali, satisfied with favour, and full of the blessings of the Lord: possess thou the west and the south.
—Deuteronomy 33:23

The word *'blessing'* in the Old Testament was formally known as *'b raka'*, which mainly symbolizes a bestowal of good, usually conceived of as material. For instance, we read in the book of Proverbs that, *"The blessing of the Lord brings wealth, and he adds no trouble to it"* **(Proverbs 10:22) NIV**.

Nevertheless, to fully understand the word blessing in its full nature, I've defined it to be God's supernatural ability placed on the inside of you, to obtain supernatural results on earth.

We know that blessings originated from God, and Jesus for that reason, illustrated this by teaching His followers the beatitudes which contains a series of blessings when excised. **(See Matthew 5:2-11)**.

Then He opened His mouth and taught them, saying: "blessed are the poor in spirit, for theirs is the kingdom of Heaven. Blessed are those who mourn, for they shall be comforted.

(Matthew 5:2-4)

When a man obeys God, the blessings from God in his life can become endless; the bible recalls Isaac prospering and continued prospering until he was prosperous. This was a result of the blessing.

The man began to prosper, and continued prospering until he became very prosperous.

(Genesis 26:13)

The NIV version reads,

The man became rich, and his wealth continued to grow until he became very wealthy.

(Genesis 26: 13) NIV

Blessings have multiple forms; it is not restricted to a specific trait. In Isaac's case, **Proverbs 10:22** is an example of the sort of blessing God released in his life—*'Wealth'*. Isaac was able to obtain supernatural results on earth wherever he went because God had blessed him to do so—"*And it came to pass, after the death of Abraham, that God blessed his son Isaac. And Isaac dwelt at Beer Lahai Roi*" **(Genesis 25:11)**.

A Christian can never truly experience the blessing from God unless the following three concepts are considered:

- Knowledge of the Blessing
- Conditional Basis
- Faith in the Blessing

Knowledge of the Blessing . . .

Firstly, without the knowledge of knowing you are blessed, and what God has blessed you to become, you can never truly experience supernatural results on earth. It's very possible to live your whole life on earth without experiencing supernatural results, although God sees you as a blessed person. Becoming a born again and stopping there doesn't fully qualify you to receiving the true blessings. You are in fact blessed by the hand of God for taking the step of giving your life to Christ. However, to go deeper and experience the true blessings, it comes with obedience, faithfulness and so on.

If God decides to bless you, He releases the blessing into the life of the physical person. This means the person has been empowered by God to transmit the bestowal for achieving favoured results. But up until the person decides to take the step in the empowerment, the blessing will just be living on the inside of them.

The first time we see the word '*blessed*' was in the book of Genesis in the first chapter, when the Lord formed the living creatures and blessed them. The bible said "*And God blessed them, saying "Be fruitful and multiply, and fill the waters in the seas, and let birds multiply on the earth.*" **(Genesis 1:22)**. The animals at this point were informed by God and knew the kind of blessing they were given. He empowered them to achieve fruitfulness and multiplication. By having this insight; they too were able to obtain blessed results.

Conditional Basis . . .

Secondly, the true blessings can only come to you on a conditional basis.

The bible reveals in the book of Deuteronomy that the blessings of God would be poured on His people that obey His commands. God had appointed His servant Moses to facilitate these commandments to His people. Although in our time, we understand that Jesus took away the old to establish the new covenant. Therefore one may argue and say "*that was the days of old*", but obedience is something that will forever be required from God; without it, it will be impossible for God's children to fully acquire the blessings.

I remember back in 2003, when it was time for me to apply to university, I had to follow normal procedures and apply through a UK system called UCAS (a central organisation through which applications are processed for entry to higher education).

Successful applicants would receive offers from the Universities that were either *'conditional'* or *'unconditional'*. A conditional offer meant that the University will offer the applicant a place if they meet certain conditions, which are usually based on their exam grades. If the applicant achieves the predicted grades or higher, then the offer will be confirmed. But if the grade was not achieved the university has the right to withdraw and on most occasions they do. On the other hand, an unconditional offer meant the applicant has met the academic requirements and whatever the results are, they are guaranteed placement.

Not so with the blessings. The blessings are based on a conditional offer. God releases the blessings when the condition of obedience is performed. An example of this is in the book of Malachi regarding our tithes; the blessing is presented on a conditional basis. If we bring the tithe to the Lord He will pour out a blessing.

Bring all the tithes into the storehouse, That there may be food in My house, and try Me now in this," Says the Lord of hosts, "If I will not open for you the windows of heaven And pour out for you such blessing, That there will not be room enough to receive it.

(Malachi 3:10)

God never said if you withhold your tithe I will still pour out such a blessing, it comes with a condition. Bring all your tithes.

As I grew in the Lord, I was never able to tithe properly; it was always irregular, presenting half the tithes, not tithing at all, tithing in the middle of the month, I just couldn't do it. On top of it, each month I had nothing remaining apart from a few lose change. Therefore, a time came when I purposed in my heart to do it right. I refused to allow my inability to manage my finances stop me from honouring God's word. So the next tithing Sunday I placed ten percent of my earnings at the altar. By the end of that same month, God somehow opened that window and was sure to pour out the blessing. I had received an increase of two hundred pounds just before that same month ended.

God commended Moses in the book of Deuteronomy to instruct the people to fully follow His commands in order to receive the blessings.

Now it shall come to pass, if you diligently obey the voice of the Lord your God, to observe carefully all His commandments which I command you today, that the Lord your God will set you high above all nations of the earth. And all these blessings shall come upon you and overtake you, because you obey the voice of the Lord your God.

(Deuteronomy 28:1-2)

Notice, the blessing God had for His people where promised on a conditional basis, the condition to diligently obey the voice of the Lord. It matches in the same way with us; if we obey the voice of God (by reading His word daily and perform what it says in truth) the blessing will be evident in our life.

Living without the knowledge of the blessing makes life ten times harder. I've seen many Christians who fail to study the bible end up misinterpreting scriptures and are therefore unable to reflect the blessings God desires to bestow on them.

The bible says in Deuteronomy 28, that the Lord will make you the head and not the tail.

And the Lord will make you the head and not the tail; you shall be above only, and not be beneath, if you heed the commandments of the Lord your God, which I command you today, and are careful to observe them.

(Deuteronomy 28:13)

Most people fail to realise this verse is connected to a requirement/condition—, *"If you heed the commandments of the Lord"*. In other words, if you obey His words/commandments, He will make you the head and not the tail. Many people don't obey the commands of God, because they don't find time to study the scriptures to know what the Lord is saying and end up praying—*"Lord you said you will make me the head and not the tail, so therefore I am the head and not the tail"*.

But it shall come to pass, if you do not obey the voice of the Lord your God, to observe carefully all His commandments and His statutes which I command you today, that all these curses will come upon you and overtake you.

(Deuteronomy 28:15)

Deuteronomy 28:44 says: *"He shall lend to you, but you shall not lend to him; he shall be the head, and you shall be the tail"*. This explains why most of us are in fact the tail and not the head, being ruled over, and not actually ruling over as God originally blessed the man Adam to do.

Looking at the story of Jacob and Esau, both were from the seed of Abraham so both were entitled to receiving some sort of blessing from their father. (*Just like us, becoming born again; we are entitled to receiving a blessing*). The bible says in the book of Galatians, *"Curse is everyone who hangs on a tree that the blessings of Abraham might come upon the Gentiles"* **(Galatians 3:13)**. Going back to the story of Jacob and Esau, somehow we see Jacob being more connected to God than Esau was. A clear indication of this is when Jacob made his brother Esau swear by the Father that he will sell to Jacob His birth right. The bible says Esau despised his birth right. *"Then Jacob gave Esau some bread and some lentil stew. He ate and drank, and then got up and left. So Esau despised his birthright"* **(Genesis 25:34) NIV**.

Esau failed to realise that in despising his birthright meant he had despised the blessings. So in reality, Esau unknowingly unloved his blessings. The fact that this happened to Esau, is not that he truly unloved the blessings as such; as we discover in the book of Hebrews and Genesis how Esau wept bitterly and in fact begged his father for another blessing. The reality was that Esau was unable to discern godly things because of his lifestyle. Esau was a natural man—*"But the natural man does not receive the things of the Spirit of God, for they are foolishness to him; nor can he know them, because they are spiritually discerned"* **(1 Corinthians 2:14)**

Esau being a natural man could have never received the blessings that he sought for from God being the type of man he was. The natural man would have never allowed him to spiritually discern and say— *"Hold on, this birthright that you are about to sell is the key to your greatness"* . . . For that reason, it was easy for him to sell his birthright because in his thinking it was foolish to him— *"And Esau said, "Look, I am about to die; so what is this birthright to me?"* **(Genesis 25:32)**. Little did he know that the birthright was a direct link to the blessing.

But Jacob on the other hand was a spiritual man and was able to discern that the birthright in fact was the key to the future, and so made a request for it— *"But Jacob said, "Sell me your birthright as of this day"* **(Genesis 25:31)**.

Jacob had the ability to judge all things rightly. *"But he who is spiritual judges all things, yet he himself is rightly judged by no one"* **(1 Corinthians 2:15)**. Jacob therefore later inherited the first born blessings, which included the blessings of being the head and not the tail. *"May nations serve you. May people bow down to you. Be the master of your brothers, and may the sons of your mother bow down to you"* **(Genesis 27:29) GWT**.

Esau on the other hand refused to obey God; he inherited a great blessing but was made the tail, to be under his brother. *"Then Isaac answered and said to Esau, "Indeed I have made him your master"* **(Genesis 27:37)**. Isaac said in Verse 39, *"Behold, your dwelling shall be of the fatness of the earth, and of the dew of heaven from above. By your sword you shall live, and you shall serve your brother"* **(Genesis 27:39-40)**.

This is an example of what can happen when you fail to obey God's word.

Joseph is another great example of being blessed with the headship blessing. Joseph by no means was Jacob's firstborn in fact Joseph at the time was the youngest out of the eleven children, even though he was Rachel's firstborn. Historically, Jacobs first born was Reuben— *"Now the sons of Jacob were twelve: the sons of Leah were Reuben, Jacobs's firstborn"* **(Genesis 35:22-23)**. But Joseph somehow began to find himself connecting with God more than his brothers. In doing this, it resulted in him becoming blessed and receiving the blessings of headship.

In **Genesis 37**, the bible recalls Joseph at the age of seventeen feeding the flock with his brothers, and on a particular day brought back a bad report to his father. Even though the bible did not make mention of what the report was, apart from it being described as something bad. Joseph found it imperative to channel the report of truth back to his father. The bible never said Joseph joined in or tried to hide what he saw from his dad but spoke out. It gives us the impression that Joseph was a trustworthy person, whilst his brothers on the other hand weren't.

This is the history of Jacob, Joseph being seventeen years old, was feeding the flock with his brothers. And the lad was with the sons of Bilhah and the sons of Zilpah, his father's wives; and Joseph brought a bad report of them to his father.

(Genesis 37:2)

A time came when Joseph received a dream from the Lord which portrayed Joseph as being the head over his family.

Now Joseph had a dream, and he told it to his brothers; and they hated him the more. So he said to them "Please hear this dream which I have dreamed: "There we were, binding sheaves in the field. Then behold, my sheaf arose and also stood upright; and indeed your sheaves stood all around and bowed down to my sheaf."And his brothers said to him, "Shall you indeed reign over us" Or shall you indeed have dominion over us?" So they hated him even more for his dreams and for his words. Then he dreamed still another dream and told it to his brothers, and said, "Look, I have dreamed another dream. And this time, the sun the moon, and the eleven stars bowed down to me." So he told it to his father and his brothers; and his father rebuked him and said to him, "What is this dream that you have dreamed? Shall your mother and I and your brothers indeed come to bow down to the earth before you? And his brother's envied him, but his father kept the matter in mind.

(Genesis 37:5-11)

Years later, Joseph's dreams came to past when his brothers came to Egypt seeking grain; they came before him with their heads bowed down.

Now Joseph was governor over the land; and it was he that sold to all the land. And Joseph's brothers came and bowed down before him with their faces to the earth.

(Genesis 42:6)

Verse 9 says, *"Then Joseph remembered the dreams which he had dreamed about them . . .*

God made Joseph the head by destiny, as Joseph from childhood listened and obeyed his father's instructions which were in line with the commandments of God. God was able to bless him. By the blessings God bestowed on Joseph, a time came when Pharaoh pronounced Joseph overseer of his house, the people, and over the entire land of Egypt.

So the advice was good in the eyes of Pharaoh and in the eyes of all his servants. And Pharaoh said to his servant, "Can we find such a one as this, a man in whom is the Spirit of God?" Then Pharaoh said to Joseph "Inasmuch as God has shown you all this, there is no one as discerning and wise as you. "You shall be over my house, and all my people shall be ruled according to your word; only in regard to the throne I will be greater than you."And pharaoh said to Joseph, "See, I have set you over the land of Egypt." Then Pharaoh took his signet ring off his hand and put it on Joseph's hand; and he clothed him in garments of fine linen and put a gold chain around his neck. And he had him ride in the second chariot which he had; and he cried out before him, "Bow the knee!" So he set him over all the land of Egypt. Pharaoh also said to Joseph, "I am Pharaoh, and without your consent no man may lift his hand or foot in all the land of Egypt.

(Genesis 41:37-44)

We see the blessing of headship working throughout his life, even in inauspicious places such as prison. Joseph was falsely accused and placed in prison, but yet the guards found it necessary to place him head over the other jailers to oversee their day to day activities.

But the LORD was with Joseph and showed him mercy and He gave him favor in the sight of the keeper of the prison. And the keeper of the prison committed to Joseph's hand all the prisoners who were in the prison; whatever they did there, it was his doing. The keeper of the prison did not look into anything that was under Joseph's authority, because the LORD was with him; and whatever he did the LORD made it prosper.

(Genesis 39:21-23)

This again was a result of obeying God, which caused the blessings of headship to remain in his life. No wonder, when the time drew near for Jacob to bless and speak into the lives of his children before dying, out of all the pronouncements that was made on his children, Joseph received much of the blessings.

By the God of your father who will help you, And by the Almighty who will bless you With blessings of heaven above, Blessings of the deep that lies beneath, blessings of the breasts and of the womb. The blessings of your father have excelled the blessings of my ancestors, Up to the utmost bound of the everlasting hills. They shall be on the head of Joseph, and on the crown of the head of him who was separate from his brothers.

(Genesis 49:25-26)

Holding firm to the Word of God growing up, I started my first career job in a law firm after graduating, having no experience in business law. I decided once again to put to practice the daily reading of the word of God by seeking out all the Christians that worked in my office and every morning before starting work email a scripture for encouragement. Not long after, I started receiving prayer requests which I gladly responded to. I would pray with them, sometimes fast with them and then believe God to come through for them. I chose to do this because the bible teaches us to encourage one another.

Therefore encourage one another and build each other up, just as in fact you are doing.

(1 Thessalonians 5:11) NIV

Later in the year, the Lord gave me an opportunity I didn't see coming. Students applied for work experience within my law firm and the successful candidates were somehow given to me to oversee their day to day work. I was allocating daily tasks to them, writing up reports and giving feedback to their schools. As I reasoned with myself, I began to see the blessings of headship working for me in an unexpected area. Within myself I knew it was a direct link of obeying God's word.

Faith in the Blessings . . .

Faith is an instrument that God wants us to continually embrace, in order for us to receive the blessings. In the days of Abraham, God pronounced an endless blessing in his life.

"I will make you a great nation; I will bless you And make your name great; And you shall be a blessing. I will bless those who bless you, And I will curse him who curses you; And in you all the families of the earth shall be blessed."

(Genesis 12:2-3)

The bible says, Abraham believed in God and it was accredited to him as righteousness. His belief allowed him to go on and develop faith in God which ended up in him being blessed.

And the scripture, foreseeing that God would justify the gentiles by faith, preached the gospel to Abraham beforehand, saying, "In you all the nations shall be blessed." So then those who are of faith are blessed with believing Abraham.

(Galatians 3:8-9)

Now, we should know that the blessing that God bestowed on Abraham, He desires to also give to us. But in order for us to experience it, we need to believe like Abraham. Faith must be displayed. The bible says *"The just shall live by faith"* **(Romans 1:17)**

Christ has redeemed us from the curse of the law, having become a curse for us (for it is written, cursed is everyone who hangs on a tree") that the blessing of Abraham might come upon the Gentiles in Christ Jesus, that we might receive the promise of the spirit through faith.

(Galatians 3:13-14)

Notice in the above verse the word we need to consider is *'might'*. It never said once Jesus hung on the tree the blessings *'will'* automatically come upon the gentiles. Although God has made it available, in order for this scripture to work effectively, faith from us is needed along with action. The bible says faith without works is dead— *"But do you want to know, O foolish man, that faith without works is dead? (James 2:20)*.

In addition to giving your life over to Christ, you have to make the choice of walking before God in total obedience to attract the blessings. To receive the blessings of Abraham, God has already constructed the right plan to align the blessings to be poured out in you, through Jesus hanging on a tree. All that's left is for us to do our part. So what is our part?

Simply to have Faith . . .

For Instance, how is it that Abraham, Isaac and Jacob were able to receive the blessing? Scripture shows us they each had a common gift in operation, *'Faith'*.

God spoke to Abraham (whom the covenant began with) saying, *"In your seed all the nations of the earth shall be blessed, because you have obeyed My voice"* **(Genesis 22:18)**. He obeyed when he was called to go out to the place which he would receive as an inheritance, not knowing where he was going **(See Hebrews 11:8)**. Abraham dwelt in the land of promise in tents with Isaac and Jacob, who were *"heirs with him of the same promise"* **(Hebrews 11:9)**. They too received the blessings by faith:

And it came to pass after the death of Abraham, that God blessed his son Isaac.

(Genesis 25:11)

By faith Isaac blessed Jacob and Esau in regard to their future.

(Hebrews 11:20)

Therefore the pronouncement of the blessings may seem like mere words, but when faith is attached, the seed of the blessings is established.

When you're blessed, God's got your back . . .

A time came when the Israelites began to move on the face of the earth in their numbers, travelled and encamped in the plains of Moab. The people of Moab where petrified because they had heard what God's people did to the Amorites. So the king of the Moabites, Balak the son of Zippor, decided the only way to stop these people was by having Balaam (a Prophet of God) curse the people.

Then he sent messengers to Balaam the son of Beor at Pethor, which is near the River in the land of the sons of his people, to call him, saying: "Look, a people has come from Egypt. See, they cover the face of the earth, and are settling next to me! "Therefore please come at once, curse this people for me, for they are too mighty for me. Perhaps I shall be able to defeat them and drive them out of the land, for I know that he whom you bless is blessed, and he whom you curse is cursed." **(Numbers 22:5-6)**

Upon this request, Balaam replied by saying, *"Lodge here tonight, and I will bring back word to you as the LORD speaks to me"* **(Numbers 22:8)**. The bible said God responded by saying, *"You shall not curse the people, for they are blessed"* **(Numbers 22:12)**.

The children of Israel where blessed, empowered from God to achieve supernatural results on earth. The blessings that God bestowed on His people were in accordance to His purpose and plan that He had for them. God made a covenant with Abraham in **Genesis 15** which made his descendants multiply, become fruitful, and posses the ability to overtake nations and territories that stood against them on their quest. As a result of these blessings, the Moabites were sick with dread.

Now Balak the son of Zippor saw all that Israel had done to the Amorites. And Moab was exceedingly afraid of the people because they were many, and Moab was sick with dread because of the children of Israel.

(Numbers 22:2-3)

But remember this could have only happened if the people carried on obeying God.

After consulting God's Prophet, Balak learnt from Balaam that God will by no means curse His people, the blessed ones. But Balaam's answer from God didn't stop Balak from trying again. Balak summoned Balaam a few more times, in an attempt to curse the people, offering various bribes such as the diviners' fee and more silver and gold. On the second occasion, Balak takes Balaam to another place from which he requested a curse to be issued on them.

Then Balak said to him, "Please come with me to another place from which you may see them; you shall see only the outer part of them, and shall not see them all; curse them for me from there."
(Numbers 23:13)

Still unsuccessful, Balak took Balaam to another place which allowed them to overlook the wasteland, hoping in fact that this time God will find error in them so a curse can be decreed.

Then Balak said to Balaam, "Please come, I will take you to another place; perhaps it will please God that you may curse them for me from there." So Balak took Balaam to the top of Peor, that overlooks the wasteland.
(Numbers 23:27-28)

However, in **Numbers 24** the bible says Balaam saw that it pleased the Lord to bless Israel and the Lord began to bestow more blessings on his people. Balak hearing this was greatly vexed and annoyed with God's Prophet.

Then Balak's anger was aroused against Balaam, and he struck his hands together; and Balak said to Balaam, "I called you to curse my enemies, and look, you have bountifully blessed them these three times!
(Numbers 24:10)

Throughout this account, we learnt that Balak tried on three separate occasions to place a curse on God's people in order to stop them. But notice, we never read from any of these events that the children of God had to run and take cover or even prayed for protection. From the scriptures perspective; it's safe to believe God's people had no idea of what was happening. Not to mention, at this specific time they were under the leadership and the dictations of Moses. Never was it mentioned within these chapters that God spoke to His Prophet (Moses) through visions and dreams that they were under any sort of attack. God most probably never bothered to make mention to Moses. This was because the people were protected by God and the blessings.

The book of Proverbs makes it quite clear that *"An undeserved curse does not come to rest"* (**Proverbs 26:2**). But I also want to submit to you, when you're blessed and walking in total obedience to God, the enemy may try and try as he tried with the Israelites, but the protection of the blessings can transform every negative utterance from the enemy into a blessing; similar to the story of Abraham and Isaac.

The bible makes mention that both men were indeed blessed from God and had married beautiful wives. However, a time came where both Abraham and Isaac's wives where in potential danger of being taken by other men. Notice that the bible never said Abraham or Isaac rose up in prayer asking God for help. In fact the only prayer that Abraham prayed was to plead with God to remove the curse that had come upon the Egyptians. Once the Lord detected the motive of Pharaoh, He immediately inflicted all sorts of great plagues within his palace. This was as a result of the blessings.

So it was, when Abram came into Egypt, that the Egyptians saw the woman, that she was very beautiful. The princes of Pharaoh also saw her and commended her to Pharaoh. And the woman was taken to Pharaoh's house. He treated Abram well for her sake. He had sheep, oxen, male donkeys, male and female servants, female donkeys, and camels. But the LORD plagued Pharaoh and his house with great plagues because of Sarai, Abram's wife. And Pharaoh called Abram and said, "What is this you have done to me? Why did you not tell me that she was your wife? "Why did you say, 'She is my sister'? I might have taken her as my wife. Now therefore, here is your wife; take her and go your way." So pharaoh commanded his men concerning him; and they sent him away, with his wife and all that he had.

(Genesis 12:14-20)

Abraham's wife was taken a second time by Abimelech, king of Gerar . . .

But God came to Abimelech in a dream by night, and said to him, "Indeed you are a dead man because of the woman whom you have taken, for she is a man's wife." But Abimelech had not come near her; and he said, "Lord, will You slay a righteous nation also? "Did he not say to me, 'She is my sister'? And she, even she herself said, 'He is my brother.' In the integrity of my heart and innocence of my hands I have done this." And God said to him in a dream, "Yes, I know that you did this in the integrity of your heart. For I also withheld you from sinning against Me; therefore I did not let you touch her. "Now therefore, restore the man's wife; for he is a prophet, and he will pray for you and you shall live. But if you do not restore her, know that you shall surely die, you and all who are yours."

(Genesis 20:3-7)

Isaac's wife Rebekah was also taken and released without a struggle . . .

So Isaac dwelt in Gerar. And the men of the place asked about his wife. And he said, "She is my sister"; for he was afraid to say, "She is my wife," because he thought, "lest the men of the place kill me for Rebekah, because she is beautiful to behold." Now it came to pass, when he had been there a long time, that Abimelech king of the Philistines looked through a window, and saw, and there was Isaac, showing endearment to Rebekah his wife. Then Abimelech called Isaac and said, "Quite obviously she is your wife; so how could you say, 'She is my sister'?"Isaac said to him, "Because I said, 'Lest I die on account of her.' "And Abimelech said, "What is this you have done to us? One of the people might soon have lain with your wife, and you would have brought guilt on us." So Abimelech charged all his people, saying, "He who touches this man or his wife shall surely be put to death."

(Genesis 26:6-11)

Obeying the Lord's commands is the key. In **Numbers 25**, as soon as God's people disobeyed God's word, we see the protection of the blessing remove and the anger of the Lord kindled.

Now Israel remained in Acacia Grove, and the people began to commit harlotry with the women of Moab. They invited the people to the sacrifices of their gods, and the people ate and bowed down to their gods. So Israel was joined to Baal of Peor, and the anger of the LORD was aroused against Israel.

(Number 25:1-3)

Blessings are one of the greatest bestowments mankind can receive from God. Therefore, it's imperative we as the recipients of the blessings do everything in our power to attract these blessings and even further blessings from God whilst we're on earth. Notice how Jacob received the firstborn blessings from his father, but by revelation found it necessary, when the opportunity came to wrestle with the Angel to obtain another blessing.

And He said, "Let Me go, for the day breaks." But he said, "I will not let You go unless You bless me!"

(Genesis 32:26)

In view of the blessings, it's important we live our daily lives in accordance to the scriptures. Peter in his account sets out guidelines on just how to achieve this.

Finally, all of you be of one mind, having compassion for one another; love as brothers, be tenderhearted, be courteous; not returning evil for evil or reviling for reviling, but on the contrary blessing, knowing that you were called to this, that you may inherit a blessing.

(1 Peter 3:8-9)

Despite what takes place on the physical, the blessing can be perceived as a sense of security, soundness and confirmation when pronounced on an individual. Joseph, when he was stripped from his coat of many colours and thrown in the pit, the blessings in him, some thirteen years later, was able to elevate him to take charge over Pharaoh's house. He was re-clothed in royal garments and given a signet ring with a gold chain. It's safe to say, once the blessings are activating in the life of the believer, it's pretty much impossible to try and hold a bless man down.

They say people who are blessed are apparently people to be pitied, but from the higher and therefore truer stance they are in fact to be envied. Isaac, who was blessed from God, was one of many who experience this first hand. The bible says because of his wealth and possessions the Philistine's envied him—*"For he had possessions of flocks and possessions of herds and a great number of servants. So the Philistines envied him"* **(Genesis 26:14)**.

At age seventeen, the Lord spoke to me saying, *"By the age of twenty five years I will honour you in marriage".* Some people I grew up with and some who were very close to me, on the outside seemed happy and verbally supportive, but on the inside it was the opposite. I then understood that when the Lord blesses you and favour goes out before you to acquire the word of the blessing, not only will you achieve that thing, people may despise you for it. Just like some who too were despised by those close to them. E.g. *Jesus, Joseph, Moses, Jacob etc.*

Not everybody can genuinely celebrate the blessed, although the bible in Romans 12 instructs us to rejoice with others. *"Rejoice with those who rejoice, and weep with those who weep"* **(Romans 12:15)**.

Abimelech noticed the blessings on Isaac and was not about to put up with it, so when the opportunity came, He told Isaac to move away—*"And Abimelech said to Isaac, "Go away from us, for you are much mightier than we"* **(Genesis 26:16)**. Later on as the blessings began to grow evident in the life of Isaac, Abimelech changed his mind, and asked for a covenant be made between them.

Then Abimelech came to him from Gerar with Ahuzzath, one of his friends, and Phichol the commander of his army. And Isaac said to them, "Why have you come to me, since you hate me and have sent me away from you?" But they said, "We have certainly seen that the LORD is with you. So we said, 'Let there now be oath between us, between you and us; and let us make a covenant with you, 'that you will do us no harm, since we have not touched you, and since we have done nothing to you but good and have sent you away in peace. You are now the blessed of the LORD.

(Genesis 26:26-29)

Abimelech now realised that being cool with Isaac will mean it will benefit him somehow. Likewise with Laban, he understood by observation and divination that Jacob was indeed blessed from God and having Jacob in his life would somehow benefit him.

But Laban said to him, 'If you will allow me to say so, I have learned by divination that the Lord has blessed me because of you;

(Genesis 30:27) NRSV

Jesus, before departing to God the Father, found it vital to bless His disciples.

And He led them out as far as Bethany, and He lifted up His hands and blessed them. Now it came to pass, while He blessed them, that He was parted from them and carried up into heaven.

(Luke 24:50-51)

CHAPTER 5

Are Men Like Trees?

He looked up and said, "I see people; they look like trees walking around.
– Mark 8:24

Trees are woody plants that normally have secondary branches which are supported by one main stem or a trunk. Trees are known to play many vital roles in our world. One being producing oxygen and reducing carbon dioxide in the atmosphere. There are different orders and families of trees in the world.

The first mentioning of a tree in the bible was in fact the fruit tree found in the book of Genesis.

Then God said, "Let the earth bring forth grass, the herb that yields seed, and the fruit tree that yields fruit according to its kind, whose seed is in itself, on the earth"; and it was so. And the earth brought forth grass, the herb that yields seed according to its kind, and the tree that yields fruit, whose seed is in itself according to its kind. And God saw that it was good. So the evening and the morning were the third day.

(Genesis 1:11-12)

God established the fruit tree to bear fruit. The fruit can then be consumed or utilized by people or even animals.

And out of the ground the LORD God made every tree grow that is pleasant to the sight and good for food.

(Genesis 2:9)

In the beginning of creation God decided to make man to dwell on earth.

Then God said, "Let Us make man in Our image, according to Our likeness.

(Genesis 1:26)

Upon making man, one part of man's purpose was to bear fruit.

Then God blessed them, and God said to them, "Be fruitful and multiply . . .

(Genesis 1:28)

Looking at the context of a *'fruit tree'*, the word *'fruit'* is a term used largely in the context of food, and we get this food or fruit by a ripened ovary or ovaries of a seed bearing plant. In a view point of *'man'* it's closely related but largely defined as a result or outcome—(*The fruit of their labor*). Therefore one of the similarities between a *'tree'* and a *'man'* are their ability to bear fruits.

The true identity of any human being is found on the inside of them. Jesus gave an illustration in the book of Matthew by saying, "*You will know them by their fruits*" (**Matthew 7:16**). He then went on likening men onto trees saying, "*Even so, every good tree bears good fruit, but a bad tree bears bad fruit*" (**Matthew 7:17**). In other words, a person is known by their fruit or by what comes out of them.

The true motives of human beings are on the inside of them. Jesus made this quite clear when He revealed in verse 15, "*Beware of false prophets, who come to you in sheep's clothing, but inwardly they are ravenous wolves*" (**Matthew 7:15**). Their bad fruit was identified when Jesus pointed out their inward part. On the outside they appear to be sheep but inwardly they were described as ravenous wolves.

As a seed is sown, in due time the farmer will reap the harvest. It's determination of becoming a good or bad fruit will be seen when it's time to blossom.

The Process . . .

Fruit trees are known to begin their process of bearing fruit after it has become old enough to blossom freely. As suspected, a number of factors can influence its ability to produce fruit. However, trees growing at a moderate rate are said to bear fruit sooner than those who grow either too quickly or too slowly. Healthy trees will produce good quality fruit, whilst weak or diseased trees produce bad, less or no fruit.

Healthy trees produce good fruit and defected trees produce bad fruits. A contributing factor for healthy trees is adequate portion of sunlight reflecting directly on them. This helps them grow nicely and strengthens their leaves. Trees that are planted near shaded buildings are known to develop quite poorly and may need to be treated with pesticides (a substance designed to kill or lessen the growth of pests that damage or interfere with the growth of crops).

Knowing all of this Jesus said, "*A good tree cannot bear bad fruit, nor can a bad tree bear good fruit*" (**Matthew 7:18**).

Where do you stand, *'good tree'* or *'bad tree'*?

The Tree Man . . .

There are times when God views us and likens us onto trees, reviewing our *fulfillment*, *enlargement* and *productivity* in life.

- **Fulfillment**—Are we fulfilling God's calling in our life? " *Therefore we also pray always for you that our God would count you worthy of this calling, and fulfill all the good pleasures of His goodness and the work of faith with power"* (**2 Thessalonians 1:11**).
- **Enlargement**—How far and wide are we spreading the gospel? Jabez asked God to enlarge his territory—"*Oh, that You would bless me indeed, and enlarge my territory"* (**1 Chronicles 4:10**).
- **Productivity**—How productive are you in producing fruit? Originally, God blessed man and said be fruitful & multiply: *"Then God blessed them, and God said to them, 'Be fruitful and multiply"* (**Genesis 1:28**).

The main reason why Jesus cursed the fig tree was because it was created to bear fruit. It's time for bearing fruit had arrived. But when Jesus came to reap its fruit, to His surprise the fig tree had not produced anything apart from leaves. For that reason, it attracted a curse from Jesus and was made to wither away.

Now in the morning, as He returned to the city, He was hungry. And seeing a fig tree by the road, He came to it and found nothing on it but leaves, and said to it, "Let no fruit grow on you ever again," Immediately the fig tree withered away.

(Matthew 21:18-19)

Another illustration is recorded in the bible where a man who owned a vineyard continuously (for three years) set out looking for fruits on the fig tree. However, on each journey he found nothing and therefore made up his mind to cut down the fig tree which was not producing.

Then he told this parable: "A man had a fig tree growing in his vineyard, and he went to look for fruit on it but did not find any. So he said to the man who took care of the vineyard, 'For three years now I've been coming to look for fruit on this fig tree and haven't found any. Cut it down! Why should it use up the soil?' "'Sir,' the man replied, 'leave it alone for one more year, and I'll dig around it and fertilize it. If it bears fruit next year, fine! If not, then cut it down".

(Luke 13:6-9) NIV

These things are written as an example to us, with the intent to warn us from becoming withered or cut down. Jesus (the mediator between God and man) is constantly interceding and pleading for us; not only for when we fall short, but when we are also not fruitful. Just like the scripture above indicates, I believe Jesus speaks to the Father on our behalf saying, *"leave it alone for one more year, and I'll dig around it and fertilize it"*, so that we can become fruitful for our Father in Heaven.

The bible warns us to be instant in season and out of season, having His word in us ready to teach others or do whatever it takes to carry on with the works of Jesus, that we can remain fruitful. Peter says, *"Preach the word! Be ready in season and out of season. Convince, rebuke, exhort, with all longsuffering and teaching"* (**2 Timothy 4:2**).

The Lord showed me once (through life and scripture), the similarities between *"men"* and *"trees"* and how they are very interchangeable. He revealed to me how He comes down to His people to receive from them the fruit which they bear. The Lord said to me, *"When I visit, many of my people are bare, almost withered trees, while others are fruitful. Teach My people to be like fruitful trees always"*.

In the below passage, the parable which Jesus shared was a vivid picture of the kind of method God uses to receive the fruits from His people.

Hear another parable: There was a certain landowner who planted a vineyard and set a hedge around it, dug a winepress in it and built a tower. And he leased it to vinedressers and went into a far country. Now when vintage-time drew near, he sent his servants to the vinedressers, that they might receive its fruit. And the vinedressers took his servants, beat one, killed one, and stoned another. Again he sent other servants, more than the first, and they did likewise to them. Then last of all he sent his son to them, saying, 'They will respect my son.' But when the vinedressers saw the son, they said among themselves, 'This is the heir. Come, let us kill him and seize his inheritance.' So they took him and cast him out of the vineyard and killed him. "Therefore, when the owner of the vineyard comes, what will he do to those vinedressers?" They said to Him, "He will destroy those wicked men miserably, and lease his vineyard to other vinedressers who will render to him the fruits in their seasons.

(**Matthew 21:33-41**)

How to Become a Fruitful Tree . . .

Being a fruitful person in life means '*becoming like a fruitful tree*'—always producing good fruits. Children of God should start seeing themselves as human trees commissioned by God to bear much good fruit. These things may appear foolish to men but to God it carries great significance.

The first steps in becoming fruitful, is having trust and hope in the Lord.

Blessed is the man who trusts in the Lord, and whose hope is the Lord. For he shall be like a tree planted by the waters, which spreads out its roots by the river, and will not fear when heat comes; But its leaf will be green, and will not be anxious in the year of drought, Nor will cease from yielding fruit.

(**Jeremiah 17:7-8**)

The second step is to learn the way of the Righteous:

Blessed is the man who walks not in the counsel of the ungodly, nor stands in the path of sinners, nor sits in the seat of the scornful; But his delight is in the law of the Lord, And in His law he meditates day and night. He shall be like a tree planted by the rivers of water, that brings forth its fruit in its season, Whose leaf also shall not wither; And whatever he does shall prosper.

(Psalms 1:3)

In the sight of God, once this is implemented in truth, God fashions and arranges you in such a way your everyday life begins to be sprout like a fruitful tree planted by the rivers of water, prospering daily, in all that you do.

In **John 15**, Jesus describes the ultimate secret on how to become fruitful. Here He reveals that abiding in Him constantly will result in a person bearing much fruit.

I am the true vine, and My Father is the vinedresser. Every branch in Me that does not bear fruit He takes away; and every branch that bears fruit He prunes, that it may bear more fruit. You are already clean because of the word which I have spoken to you. Abide in Me, and I in you. As the branch cannot bear fruit of itself, unless it abides in the vine, neither can you, unless you abide in Me." I am the vine, you are the branches. He who abides in Me, and I in him, bears much fruit; for without Me you can do nothing. If anyone does not abide in Me, he is cast out as a branch and is withered; and they gather them and throw them into the fire, and they are burned. If you abide in Me, and My words abide in you, you will ask what you desire, and it shall be done for you. By this My Father is glorified, that you bear much fruit; so you will be My disciples.

(John 15:1-8)

Most Christians can recognize when they're in a pit. In fact, most Christians can relate well to the story of Joseph. But one of the most philosophical reasons as to why Joseph was victorious with God and man was in fact because he bore much fruit, in accordance to the fruit of the spirit which Apostle Paul revealed to us in the book of Galatians: "*But the fruit of the Spirit is love, joy, peace, longsuffering, kindness, goodness, faithfulness, gentleness, self-control*" (**Galatians 5:22-23**).

Before Joseph went into captivity he was extremely fruitful and more so during captivity. Look how strongly Joseph exhibited each one of the fruits of the Spirit in his own life.

Love	Despite all that his brothers had done to him, Joseph still loved them unconditionally
Joy	Joseph exhibited joy even when things weren't looking bright for him
Peace	Joseph found peace even when he was in prison and was placed in charge over other prisoners

Longsuffering	Despite affliction, Joseph remained a lover of God and endured hardship
Kindness	Joseph showed pity on Pharaoh's officers and interpreted their dreams
Goodness	Joseph gathered abundance of food in Egypt
Faithfulness	Joseph kept the laws of God at the peak of his heart
Gentleness	Despite the resentment Joseph received from people, he remained gentle
Self-control	Joseph was able to demonstrate self-control over Potiphar's wife

In God's sight, Joseph was considered a fruitful tree. The God's Word Translation bible says: *"[Joseph] is a fruitful tree, a fruitful tree by a spring, with branches climbing over a wall"* (**Genesis 49:22**) **GWT**.

God Can Destroy Your Tree . . .

Earlier we read in **Luke 13:6-9**, how the landowner intended to cut down the non fruitful trees. There are times when God can use the tree dialogue to represent us. God is known to send rain on the righteous as well as the unrighteous; that's the love He has for us. The bible reveals that God takes no pleasure in the death of the wicked wanting all men to turn from evil—*"Say to them: 'As I live,' says the Lord God,' I have no pleasure in the death of the wicked, but that the wicked turn from his way and live. Turn, turn from your evil ways! For why should you die, O house of Israel?"* (**Ezekiel 33:11**).

Joseph was pronounced a fruitful tree because of the fruits he bore in his life. Unlike Joseph, God saw King Nebuchadnezzar as a tree bearing bad fruits.

These were the visions of my head while on my bed: I was looking, and behold, A tree in the midst of the earth, And its height was great. The tree grew and became strong; Its height reached to the heavens, And it could be seen to the ends of all the earth. Its leaves were lovely, Its fruit abundant, And in it was food for all. The beasts of the field found shade under it, The birds of the heavens dwelt in its branches, And all flesh was fed from it."I saw in the visions of my head while on my bed, and there was a watcher, a holy one, coming down from heaven. He cried aloud and said thus:' Chop down the tree and cut off its branches, Strip off its leaves and scatter its fruit. Let the beasts get out from under it, And the birds from its branches. Nevertheless leave the stump and roots in the earth, Bound with a band of iron and bronze, In the tender grass of the field. Let it be wet with the dew of heaven, And let him graze with the beasts On the grass of the earth. Let his heart be changed from that of a man, Let him be given the heart of a beast, And let seven times pass over him.' This decision is by the decree of the watchers, And the sentence by the word of the holy ones, In order that the living may know That the Most High rules in the kingdom of men, Gives it to whomever He will, And sets over it the lowest of men.

(Daniel 4:10-17)

God had made this decree over the king's life, as a result of him having pride, taking the glory of God, and refusing to recognize God as the solitary purpose of him triumphing in life. As a result, God sought to remove him temporally from his position by having his tree cut down which affected him directly on earth.

The tree that you saw, which grew and became strong, whose height reached to the heavens and which could be seen by all the earth, whose leaves were lovely and its fruit abundant, in which was food for all, under which the beasts of the field dwelt, and in whose branches the birds of the heaven had their home— it is you, O king, who have grown and become strong; for your greatness has grown and reaches to the heavens, and your dominion to the end of the earth. And inasmuch as the king saw a watcher, a holy one, coming down from heaven and saying, 'Chop down the tree and destroy it, but leave its stump and roots in the earth, bound with a band of iron and bronze in the tender grass of the field; let it be wet with the dew of heaven, and let him graze with the beasts of the field, till seven times pass over him'; this is the interpretation, O king, and this is the decree of the Most High, which has come upon my lord the king: They shall drive you from men, your dwelling shall be with the beasts of the field, and they shall make you eat grass like oxen. They shall wet you with the dew of heaven, and seven times shall pass over you, till you know that the Most High rules in the kingdom of men, and gives it to whomever He chooses." And inasmuch as they gave the command to leave the stump and roots of the tree, your kingdom shall be assured to you, after you come to know that Heaven rules. Therefore, O king, let my advice be acceptable to you; break off your sins by being righteous, and your iniquities by showing mercy to the poor. Perhaps there may be a lengthening of your prosperity.

(Daniel 4:20-27)

We are warned to bear good fruit, much fruit. In the scripture above, the illustration of the tree represented King Nebuchadnezzar, his greatness, his power, and his splendour. He bore much fruit, and as a result many people reaped from his tree. The bible says in verse 12 of this Chapter, *"Its fruit abundant, and in it was food for all".* Even birds nested in his branches. However the fruits which he bore began to displease God and he was therefore warned that his tree would be cut down if a change doesn't come.

John also indicated in his teachings that every bad tree will be cut down: *"The ax is already at the root of the trees, and every tree that does not produce good fruit will be cut down and thrown into the fire"* **(Luke 3:9) NIV**.

Pharaoh had a great and powerful kingdom in Egypt, but the fall of Pharaoh and Egypt came about through prideful acts. Just like King Nebuchadnezzar, Pharaoh and Egypt were also issued with a decree to be cut down like great trees.

Now it came to pass in the eleventh year, in the third month, on the first day of the month, that the word of the LORD came to me, saying,"Son of man, say to Pharaoh king of Egypt and to his multitude:' Whom are you like in your greatness? Indeed Assyria was a cedar in Lebanon, With fine branches that shaded the forest, And of high stature; And its top was among the thick boughs. The waters made it grow; Underground waters gave it height, With their rivers running around the place where it was planted, And sent out rivulets to all the trees of the field.' Therefore its height was exalted above all the trees of the field; Its boughs were multiplied, And its branches became long because of the abundance of water, As it sent them out. All the birds of the heavens made their nests in its boughs; Under its branches all the beasts of the field brought forth their young; And in its shadow all great nations made their home.' Thus it was beautiful in greatness and in the length of its branches, Because its roots reached to abundant waters. The cedars in the garden of God could not hide it; The fir trees were not like its boughs, And the chestnut trees were not like its branches; No tree in the garden of God was like it in beauty. I made it beautiful with a multitude of branches, So that all the trees of Eden envied it, That were in the garden of God.' "Therefore thus says the Lord GOD: 'Because you have increased in height, and it set its top among the thick boughs, and its heart was lifted up in its height, therefore I will deliver it into the hand of the mighty one of the nations, and he shall surely deal with it; I have driven it out for its wickedness. And aliens, the most terrible of the nations, have cut it down and left it; its branches have fallen on the mountains and in all the valleys; its boughs lie broken by all the rivers of the land; and all the peoples of the earth have gone from under its shadow and left it.' On its ruin will remain all the birds of the heavens, And all the beasts of the field will come to its branches— 'So that no trees by the waters may ever again exalt themselves for their height, nor set their tops among the thick boughs, that no tree which drinks water may ever be high enough to reach up to them. 'For they have all been delivered to death, To the depths of the earth, Among the children of men who go down to the Pit.' "Thus says the Lord GOD: 'In the day when it went down to hell, I caused mourning. I covered the deep because of it. I restrained its rivers, and the great waters were held back. I caused Lebanon to mourn for it, and all the trees of the field wilted because of it. I made the nations shake at the sound of its fall, when I cast it down to hell together with those who descend into the Pit; and all the trees of Eden, the choice and best of Lebanon, all that drink water, were comforted in the depths of the earth. They also went down to hell with it, with those slain by the sword; and those who were its strong arm dwelt in its shadows among the nations.'To which of the trees in Eden will you then be likened in glory and greatness? Yet you shall be brought down with the trees of Eden to the depths of the earth; you shall lie in the midst of the uncircumcised, with those slain by the sword. This is Pharaoh and all his multitude,' says the Lord GOD."

(Ezekiel 31:1-18)

Ezekiel 31:18 talks about the cutting down of a tree which represented Pharaoh and his multitudes. We can conclude from the description of the tree that it was one of the greatest trees God had created. **Verse 9** states, *"I made it beautiful with a multitude of branches, so that all the trees of Eden envied it, That were in the garden of God".*

In the physical, Egypt was a mighty nation. Even to this day its landmarks still remain the focal point of discovery by Egyptologist and many other people around the world. Nevertheless, God issued a decree to end Pharaoh's kingdom forever, which would come in a spiritual form of a tree being cut down.

I now understand that God, the '*True Vinedresser*' (**John 15:1**), will come and receive the fruits from your tree. How great and wonderful will it be to Him that He finds many good fruits ready to be rendered unto Him on His visits?

Your tree is important, although it is not really a physical tree. But it is a type of expression the Lord uses to narrate to us.

The Lord had a secret name for the people of Judah '*a green olive tree*'—"*The LORD called your name, Green Olive Tree, Lovely and of Good Fruit*" (**Jeremiah 11:16**). For this reason, one should find it very necessary to keep confessing the following:

"*I am like a fruitful tree bearing much fruit in and out of season unto the glory of GOD*"

A clear example of this is in the book of Psalms—"*But I am like a large olive tree in God's house. I trust the mercy of God forever and ever*" (**Psalms 52:8**).

The enemy may try and attempt to cause you to bear no fruit in life which can affect you in the land of the living. There was a time in the bible, when the enemies of Jeremiah conspired to kill him. God being faithful revealed the plot to Jeremiah so he could be saved.

Now the LORD gave me knowledge of it, and I know it; for You showed me their doings. But I was like a docile lamb brought to the slaughter; and I did not know that they had devised schemes against me, saying, "Let us destroy the tree with its fruit, and let us cut him off from the land of the living, that his name may be remembered no more."

(**Jeremiah 11:18-19**)

Are men trees? Certainly not! But God expects us to bear much fruit like trees.

CHAPTER 6

Engage in Spiritual Warfare

BLESSED be the LORD my Rock, Who trains my hands for war, And my fingers for battle.
– Psalms 144:1

The word *'Engage'* can be described in a number of ways. Below are a few examples.

- Encounter
- Fight
- Interested
- Connect
- Earnest
- Involved

The word *'warfare'* normally refers to the conduct of conflict between opponents. It usually involves escalation of aggression from the proverbial *'war of words'* between politicians and diplomats, to full-scale armed conflicts waged until one side accepts defeat, or peace terms are agreed on.

Warfare between groups, or even more so between military organizations, requires a degree of planning and application of military strategy to be conducted effectively in reaching their assumed objectives and goals.

In Christian terms, spiritual warfare could either be seen as a short or long term battle between a believer and an evil spirit(s) waged until one side is defeated or destroyed. For the believer, his or her opponent (evil spirit(s) is not often seen through the psychical eye, but is believed to exist, and at times perceived to be in close radius when praying.

Apostle Paul wrote a letter to the church in Ephesians, stating the importance of putting on the full armor of God—*"Finally, my brethren, be strong in the Lord and in the power of His might. Put on the whole armor of God, that you may be able to stand against the wiles of the devil"* **(Ephesians 6:10-11)**.

By the next verse, Apostle Paul identified who exactly we are up against.

For we do not wrestle against flesh and blood, but against principalities, against powers, against the rulers of the darkness of this age, against spiritual hosts of wickedness in the heavenly places.
(Ephesians 6:10-12).

The need to engage in spiritual warfare through prayers is quite important in the life of every born again Christian. The bible warns us to stay alert and watch out for our enemy who seeks to overcome us—"*Be self-controlled and alert. Your enemy the devil prowls around like a roaring lion looking for someone to devour*" **(1 Peter 5:8)**. In other words, Satan goes around like a ravenous beast looking for one Christian at a time to demolish. If you understand the hunting tactics of a lion, you will have a basic understanding of how Satan maps out his attacks.

Lions are known to only run fast in short burst, needing to be close to their prey before they can start their attack. Lions when attacking lay low, blend with their environment, spy out the field, and calculate how near they need to be to catch their prey; all before they make their first move. Like lions, Satan doesn't just get up and attack disorderly. Satan prowls first seeing who he may attack—*Who's lacking in faith, who's angry with their brother* etc. Upon his prowling, he is able to draw near and strike; very similar to the art of a lion.

A large amount of successful lion attacks are said to take place when visibility is reduced—during night times, and when they discover a place to hide. The term *'reduced visibility'* is very interesting. I was once conversing with my pastor when he said, *"The power of the enemy lies within his ability to hide his attacks from us"*. This makes sense, if we knew how Satan planned to attack us, would we allow it to happen? Certainly not!

Engaging in spiritual warfare encourages us as Christians to always be on the *'offense'* rather than *'defense'*. If a fight should occur, we should rather be the one to ignite it rather than to defend it. We should be trained like soldiers, ready to chase the enemy—not running from the enemy. That's why David, at a particular time in his life was thankful to God for training him for battle—*"Blessed be the LORD my Rock, Who trains my hands for war, And my fingers for battle"* **(Psalms 144:1)**.

As Christians, we are told not to be ignorant of the devices of the enemy—"*lest Satan should take advantage of us; for we are not ignorant of his devices*" **(2 Corinthians 2:11)**. Although Apostle Paul came from the view point of forgiving the offender lest Satan takes advantage, I believe this scripture can go a long way. If we are able to come to a place in our lives where we know what the enemy will do next, eventually, he will have less and less room to operate strategically in our lives.

In the body of Christ, you may have heard the phrase, *'God reveals to redeem'*. The understanding behind this is that God reveals to his children via dreams, sermons in Church or even through your daily reading of the bible, plans the enemy has made in an attempt to attack us.

How are These Fights Provoked . . . ?

The ultimate factor of how these fights are provoked is simply the devil hates all God's people and seeks to make war with them and destroy them.

And the dragon was enraged with the woman, and he went to make war with the rest of her offspring, who keep the commandments of God and have the testimony of Jesus Christ.

(Revelation 12:17)

Evil spirits are sometimes assigned from the kingdom of darkness to bring to pass various evil applications that can diminish your life without you even having an idea that you're being attacked. We are now aware of generational and self afflicted curses which all can provoke the battle.

How Do We End Up On The Spiritual Battle Field . . . ?

Physical battle fields are grounds where battles are fought. At times God can permit His children to enter into spiritual battle fields through dreams or intense prayer, either to receive something or do something. Other times a demon ensnares and holds God's people there against their will.

A time came when God revealed a series of revelations to Ezekiel. On one occasion, God revealed to Ezekiel that a group of men were secretly plotting to kill God's people.

Then the Spirit lifted me up and brought me to the gate of the house of the LORD that faces east. There at the entrance of the gate were twenty-five men, and I saw among them Jaazaniah son of Azzur and Pelatiah son of Benaiah, leaders of the people. The LORD said to me, "Son of man, these are the men who are plotting evil and giving wicked advice in this city. They say, 'Will it not soon be time to build houses? This city is a pot, and we are the meat.' Therefore prophesy against them; prophesy, son of man." Then the Spirit of the LORD came upon me, and he told me to say: "This is what the LORD says: That is what you are saying, O house of Israel, but I know what is going through your mind. You have killed many people in this city and filled its streets with the dead. "Therefore this is what the Sovereign LORD says: The bodies you have thrown there are the meat and this city is the pot, but I will drive you out of it.

(Ezekiel 11:1-7) NIV

God was about to pronounce judgment on a group of leaders in Israel for the wickedness they were doing. God's people were under a severe spiritual attack that had manifested physically, which resulted in a string of attacks and deaths in a particular city. From the bible's point of view, the cause of the attack was unknown to His people. Death kept on recurring throughout the city, until the Lord revealed it to the Prophet Ezekiel in the vision.

The battle field here was the city, but in the realms of the spirit, God saw it as a pot. God's people, who were being attacked, were described as meat ready to be eaten. God used Ezekiel's prophesy to wage war against the evil which had been secretly plotted in the city.

This city will not be a pot for you, nor will you be the meat in it; I will execute judgment on you at the borders of Israel. And you will know that I am the LORD, for you have not followed my decrees or kept my laws but have conformed to the standards of the nations around you." Now as I was prophesying, Pelatiah son of Benaiah died. Then I fell face down and cried out in a loud voice, "Ah, Sovereign LORD! Will you completely destroy the remnant of Israel?"

(Ezekiel 11:11-13) NIV

God was totally against the killing in the city and in order to stop it, God revealed it to His servant and used what I call, *'war of words'* in a form of prophecy to wage battle until this thing ceased.

Evil spirits can operate by observing times and seasons, and are not restricted if its day or night. Notice the Psalmist said, *"Thou shalt not be afraid for the terror by night; nor for the arrow that flieth by day; Nor for the pestilence that walketh in darkness; nor for the destruction that wasteth at noonday"* **(Psalms 91:5-6) KJV**.

The people that decided to crash the planes into the Twin Towers on Tuesday 11th September 2001, neither decided to do so minutes or hours before. A carefully detailed plan would have needed to be constructed; how they were going to do it, who they would use, dates and times etc.

Jesus spoke to the multitude explaining the value of planning ahead of war—*"Or what king, going to make war against another king, does not sit down first and consider whether he is able with ten thousand to meet him who comes against him with twenty thousand?"* **(Luke 14:31)**.

Instructions in relation to a firm with many employees, usually comes from the CEO/ Founder. Satan, who is the father of lies and murderer from the beginning **(John 8:44)**, transfers information down to his cohorts to execute his plans and devices against Christians.

God protects us most times without us knowing it. For example, Job had a hedge around him which stopped Satan from harming him **(Job 1:10)**. In other times, God may chose to show us.

Spiritual attacks can occur in various forms. Some may experience something I call *'tangible'* attacks, where people see themselves leaving their own body to stand in front of wizard and witches to be tormented, whilst others are *'intangible'*, being tormented without the person feeling or knowing it.

Demons are able to walk with you from childhood to adulthood, ensuring demonic devises planted for many years in one's life, are working effectively. Jesus encountered one of these experiences in Mark 9.

Then they brought him to Him. And when he saw Him, immediately the spirit convulsed him, and he fell on the ground and wallowed, foaming at the mouth. So He asked his father, "How long has this been happening to him?" And he said, "From childhood. "And often he has thrown him both into the fire and into the water to destroy him. But if You can do anything, have compassion on us and help us.

(Mark 9:20-22)

Demons are able to speak destruction from their kingdom into your life.

Demons are able to use the earth, the sun, the moon, etc. as instruments to uphold their plans against you. Ultimately, when you're born into the world you become a target, and now you've given your life to Christ, welcome to the battle field . . .

You need to be ready to attack and cast them out of your life, and also to help others. God is saying in our times, rather than always being on the defensive side, always having to pray after you've had a disturbing dream, waking up in the morning crying, cancelling attacks,—*it's time to rise up and declare war!*

Raise the war cry, you nations, and be shattered! Listen, all you distant lands. Prepare for battle, and be shattered! Prepare for battle, and be shattered! Devise your strategy, but it will be thwarted; propose your plan, but it will not stand, for God is with us.

(Isaiah 8:9-10) NIV

During the time of Moses, after the Lord delivered His children out of the land of Egypt, Moses and the children of Israel raised a song to the Lord, based on His power and might when they saw God operate on their behalf. They referred to God as a God of War—*"The LORD is a man of war; The LORD is His name" (***Exodus 15:3)**.

The Lord God is not a God who just sits on a big throne throwing out commands to His Angels all day. God is a very active God who's always engaging in warfare. The NIV version reads, *"The LORD is a warrior"* **(Exodus 15:3) NIV**.

The Book of Isaiah says, *"Behold, the LORD rides on a swift cloud, And will come into Egypt; The idols of Egypt will totter at His presence, And the heart of Egypt will melt in its midst"* **(Isaiah 19:1)**. Warfare as we now know requires a degree of tactical planning. In **Verse 3** of the same scripture, the bible declares that God will destroy the tactical plans the enemy upholds when He comes to wage war.

And the spirit of the Egyptians within them will become exhausted and emptied out and will fail, and I will destroy their counsel and confound their plans; and they will seek counsel from the idols and the sorcerers, and from those having familiar spirits (the mediums) and the wizards.

(Isaiah 19:3) AMP

In the earlier life of Abram, he was confronted with a situation where he received word that his nephew had been taken captive by surrounding nations.

Then one who had escaped came and told Abram the Hebrew, for he dwelt by the terebinth trees of Mamre the Amorite, brother of Eshcol and brother of Aner; and they were allies with Abram. Now when Abram heard that his brother was taken captive, he armed his three hundred and eighteen trained servants who were born in his own house, and went in pursuit as far as Dan. He divided his forces against them by night, and he and his servants attacked them and pursued them as far as Hobah, which is north of Damascus. So he brought back all the goods, and also brought back his brother Lot and his goods, as well as the women and the people.

(Genesis 14:13-16)

Although we know from **Chapters 12** and **13**, Abram received his blessing from the Lord; notice how the bible reveals the tactic he used to rescue his nephew. The bible says he armed three hundred and eighteen trained servants who were born in his own house for war. From this we can see that Abram carefully selected trained servants and armed them for battle. He then led the army forth to Dan and diplomatically divided his forces against the enemy by night. He then was able to attack and purse the enemy, eventually overpowering them and freeing both the people and all that had been taken captive. Abram was the chief commander of the battle. He engaged in warfare to bring about victory.

The bible speaks of the battles David encountered. In particular, the men who were with David engaging in warfare, and how God was using them to win battles.

Benaiah was the son of Jehoiada, the son of a valiant man from Kabzeel, who had done many deeds. He had killed two lion-like heroes of Moab. He also had gone down and killed a lion in the midst of a pit on a snowy day. And he killed an Egyptian, a man of great height, five cubits tall. In the Egyptian's hand there was a spear like a weaver's beam; and he went down to him with a staff, wrested the spear out of the Egyptian's hand, and killed him with his own spear. These things Benaiah the son of Jehoiada did, and won a name among three mighty men. Indeed he was more honored than the thirty, but he did not attain to the first three. And David appointed him over his guard.

(1 Chronicles 11:22)

We know that our fight is not against flesh and blood (physical human beings), but against principalities and powers. However, asking God to bless you with the strength and the spiritual ability to overthrow demons (as He empowered Benaiah physically to overthrow his enemies) could be your first prayer point.

The scripture below speaks of other men who came to aid David in battles.

Some Gadites joined David at the stronghold in the wilderness, mighty men of valor, men trained for battle, who could handle shield and spear, whose faces were like the faces of lions, and were as swift as gazelles on the mountains.

(1 Chronicles 12:8)

The bible says the men that joined David were swift as Gazelles; Gazelles are known to be swift animals able to maintain speed as high as 50 miles per hour (80km/h). These were the type of men that were around David winning battles. Ask the Lord to make your spirit as *'swift as a Gazelle'*.

God has an army. The term *'Army'* has various definitions such as, a vast multitude, a collection or body of men armed for war, a collective group united for the same purpose, etc. Why do you think the Lord found it necessary to have an army? The answer is simple, because God is a God of war. The bible reveals how David's army grew until it became like the army of God.

And they helped David against the bands of raiders, for they were all mighty men of valor, and they were captains in the army. For at that time they came to David day by day to help him, until it was a great army, like the army of God.

(1 Chronicles 12:21-22)

God being the *'All Powerful God'* is God all by Himself! **(Psalms 86:10),** but God is a Warrior who trains His Soldiers for war just as He trained David.

What Are My Weapons . . . ?

"For the weapons of our warfare are not carnal but mighty in God for pulling down of strongholds" **(2 Corinthians 10:4).**

Below are some of the mighty weapons that can be used in battling against the enemy.

- Word of God
- The name JESUS
- Blood of Jesus
- Angels of God
- Speaking in Tongues
- Your own Tongue (your decree)
- Prophesy
- God's divine Power
- The Leading of the Holy Spirit
- The Holy Spirit's *'Fire'* and *'Wind'*

Like David's men, we too need to be experts in war with every kind of weapon for war. They knew how to keep ranks and battle formations, and were armed with shields and spears.

Of Zebulun there were fifty thousand who went out to battle, expert in war with all weapons of war, stouthearted men who could keep ranks; of Naphtali one thousand captains, and with them thirty-seven thousand with shield and spear; of the Danites who could keep battle formation, twenty-eight thousand six hundred; of Asher, those who could go out to war, able to keep battle formation, forty thousand; of the Reubenites and the Gadites and the half-tribe of Manasseh, from the other side of the Jordan, one hundred and twenty thousand armed for battle with every kind of weapon of war.

(1 Chronicles 12:33-37)

How Do I Win the Battle . . . ?

The victory has already been given when Jesus went to the cross at Calvary. *"Having disarmed principalities and powers, He made a public spectacle of them, triumphing over them in it"* **(Colossians 2:15).** However, Jesus expects us to win the battles to complement the victory given to us. Amen.

In **Luke 9** we see Jesus giving power to His disciples over all scorpions and evil: *"Then He called His twelve disciples together and gave them power and authority over all demons, and to cure diseases"* **(Luke 9:1).**

The bible says, *"Therefore, prepare your minds for action"* **(1 Peter 1:13) NIV.** You need an action mind set as we know that when changes begin it starts from the mind. Pray that your mind will be set for battle. When you have done this, the bible says, *"Be self-controlled and alert"* **(1 Peter 5:8) NIV.** As stated earlier, your enemy (the devil) prowls around like a roaring lion looking someone to devour. Being self-controlled and alert are important for winning the battle. When you do this, nothing should take you by surprise. After all, the bible says, *"The secret things belong to the LORD our God"* **(Deuteronomy 29:29).**

Remember, you're in a spiritual battle field.

Quick revelation God just put in my Spirit—no wonder why Peter, in the garden of Gethsemane, was quick on the mark to attack the soldiers when they came to arrest Jesus. He cut off the right ear of one of the soldiers called *'Malchus'.* We know soldiers are military armed forces, who've gone through a series of training for battle. But yet, Peter the fisherman, was able to pull a sword and swiftly strike the ear of the soldier.

After all of this, invite the Holy Spirit to show you all truths. This will help you identify who you are facing and where they are operating from.—*"But when he, the Spirit of truth, comes, he will guide you into all truth. He will not speak on his own; he will speak only what he hears, and he will tell you what is yet to come"* **(John 16:13) NIV.**

Use your weapons given to you from God, and begin to pray consistently time after time, as often as the Lord leads you. The victory will be yours. I say to all, **"Engage in Spiritual Warfare".**

CHAPTER 7

Men Rejects, But God Accepts

Coming to Him as to a living stone, rejected indeed by men, but chosen by God and precious
—1 Peter 2:4

'Reject' or *'Rejection'* could be defined as a refusal to grant a request or demand, whilst the word *'Accept'* is normally used when something or someone takes or receives something offered with approval.

Men as we know have been created in the image of God, in His likeness. Being created in the image and likeness of God, it's safe to say our image bears similarities as with God's. Just by reviewing **Genesis 1**, we learn that God is a God who moves, speaks and sees. All of which God has designed men to do.

Movement

And the Spirit of God was hovering over the face of the waters . . . (**Genesis 1:2**)

Speaks

Then God said, "Let there be light" . . . (**Genesis 1:3**)

Sight

And God saw the light . . . (**Genesis 1:4**)

The author of the book of Hebrews, by revelation, revealed that Jesus is said to be the express image of God.

Who being the brightness of His glory and the express image of His person, and upholding all things by the word of His power, when He had by himself purged our sins, sat down at the right hand of the Majesty on high.

(Hebrews 1:3)

Although this is apparent, there yet seems to be some underlining facts that obviously distinguish God from all men. Isaiah said God's thoughts and ways are not like men.

"For My thoughts are not your thoughts, Nor are your ways My ways," says the LORD. "For as the heavens are higher than the earth. So are My ways higher than your ways, and My thoughts than your thoughts"

(Isaiah 55:8-9)

This leads us to the final chapter of this book—*'Men reject but God accepts'*. A time came when the Lord called Samuel to set off on a Journey to anoint one of the sons of Jesse the Bethlehemite, in place of King Saul. Being given instructions from God, Samuel was able to announce to the villagers that the reason for his visit was to offer a sacrifice to God.

And Samuel said, "How can I go? If Saul hears of it, he will kill me." But the Lord said, "Take a heifer with you, and say, 'I have come to sacrifice to the Lord.

(1 Samuel 16:2)

Upon doing this, the Lord then told him to invite Jesse and his sons to the sacrifice, and in that moment the Lord will name among Jesse's sons who God's anointed is. Samuel having followed the word of God entirely, in preparation for the meal, ordered his guests to be sanctified.

And he said, "Peaceably; I have come to sacrifice to the LORD. Sanctify yourselves, and come with me to the sacrifice." Then he consecrated Jesse and his sons, and invited them to the sacrifice.

(1 Samuel 16:5)

Samuel, being a man, immediately glanced at one of Jesse's sons, seeing his outer appearance, concluded that this must be the Lord's anointed. But the Lord told Samuel He has refused him.

So it was, when they came, that he looked at Eliab and said, "Surely the LORD'S anointed is before Him!" But the LORD said to Samuel, "Do not look at his appearance or at his physical stature, because I have refused him. For the LORD does not see as man sees; for a man looks at the outward appearance, but the LORD looks at the heart."

(1 Samuel 16:6-7)

After Samuel was corrected by the Lord, he patiently waited for who the Lord had named. But to his surprise, all of Jesse's sons had came and passed and yet the Lord had not spoken to him. Samuel then asked Jesse *"is this all your sons?"*

So Jesse called Abinadab, and made him pass before Samuel. And he said, "Neither has the LORD chosen this one." Then Jesse made Shammah pass by. And he said, "Neither has the LORD chosen this one." Thus Jesse made seven of his sons pass before Samuel. And Samuel said to Jesse, "The LORD has not chosen these." And Samuel said to Jesse, "Are all the young men here?" Then he said, "There remains yet the youngest, and there he is, keeping the sheep." And Samuel said to Jesse, "Send and bring him. For we will not sit down till he comes here." So he sent and brought him in. Now he was ruddy, with bright eyes, and good-looking. And the LORD said, "Arise, anoint him; for this is the one!"

Then Samuel took the horn of oil and anointed him in the midst of his brothers; and the Spirit of the LORD came upon David from that day forward. So Samuel arose and went to Ramah.

(1 Samuel 16:8-13)

David was so rejected, it was almost as if he had been forgotten and considered unapproved for such family gatherings. On the physical aspect, his family may have seen him as the baby, being the youngest in the family. They therefore made up their minds that David had no need to attend the feast and perhaps his day job of keeping the flocks was far more important than being invited to the ambiguous sacrifice. Remember, David like the rest of his brothers was called to the feast by God, but for some unknown reason David failed to receive his invite. However, rejection was the key ingredient that was in operation here. This is exactly how rejection works, when you're denied something you potentially qualify for.

There is a high possibility that his father never even bothered to hand David his invite. We learn from the scriptures that Jesse and his sons were sanctified and consecrated in preparation for the meal; while David had to be fetched from the field as soon as Samuel discovered there was one missing from the feast. It's also a possibility that David had missed out on being consecrated with his brothers. As a parent, you would automatically think because God's Prophet was in town and had made reservations to feast in your home, you would want to have your sons present in order to receive from the Man of God.

When you're in God's will and such incidents occur it's just a clear indication of how powerful God's plans for you are. Men will *'reject'* you but God will soon *'elect'* you. Satan was not afraid for David's brothers to be anointed and appointed king over Israel, as long as he kept David the real deal away and forgotten.

We know that David was a man after God's own heart— *"But now your kingdom shall not continue. The Lord has sought for Himself a man after His own heart* **(1 Samuel 13:14)**.

Could this have been said about David's brothers if they were to be named king over Israel?

Could any of David's brothers write prolific poetry in the same mannerism as David?

Could any of his brothers play the harp so beautifully that even evil spirits would be driven away?

These are some of the questions that come to mind as to why the enemy will be afraid for men to accept someone like David. As a result, today we read a large portion of David's works in the book of Psalms.

Moses went through something similar. The bible makes it plain that men rejected Moses but God had accepted him. A time came when Moses began to have a change of mind and a transforming heart as to who he really was. He was slowly but surely renouncing his Egyptian citizenship— *"By faith Moses, when he became of age, refused to be called the son of Pharaoh's daughter"* **(Hebrews 11:24)**.

God had begun to drop small revelations in the spirit of Moses to connect him to his destiny.

"Now when he was forty years old, it came into his heart to visit his brethren, the children of Israel. "And seeing one of them suffer wrong, he defended and avenged him who was oppressed, and stuck down the Egyptian. "For he supposed that his brethren would have understood that God would deliver them by his hand, but they did not understand.

(Acts 7:23-25)

Moses was misunderstood through his self-imposed actions. Being pressed by his transforming heart, he found himself freely walking in the plains of Egypt the next day. This time he tried to reconcile two Hebrew men who were fighting.

"And the next day he appeared to two of them as they were fighting, and tried to reconcile them, saying 'Men, you are brethren; why do you wrong one another?' "But he who did his neighbor wrong pushed him away, saying, 'Who made you a ruler and a judge over us? Do you want to kill me as you did the Egyptian yesterday?

(Acts 7:26-28)

The bible says at this point Moses fled and dwelt in Midian and sometime after the Lord appeared to him and confirmed the calling on his life.

'Then the LORD said to him, "Take your sandals of your feet, for the place where you stand is holy ground. "I have seen the oppression of My people who are in Egypt; I have heard their groaning and I have come down to deliver them. And now come, I will send you to Egypt." "This Moses whom they rejected, saying, 'Who made you a ruler and a judge?' is the one God sent to be a ruler and a deliverer by the hand of the Angel who appeared to him in the bush.

(Acts 7:33-35)

Certain men in the camp of the Hebrews had no idea who would help them if God had answered their prayers; but whoever God would send, they were pretty sure Moses was the last person on earth to be considered fit for the job. From their eyes, he was not only now an Egyptian, but was a perfect example of an Israelite reject.

Sometimes we may feel we have fallen into this category when the outer appearance doesn't necessarily correlate with men's expectations. People close to us may forget us, reject us, or even try and disregard our existence and capabilities, to accomplish something that the Lord has placed in us. But men's rejections are never the final word, but God who looks on the inside (*at the heart of men*), is able to confirm who is on His elect list.

Having being accepted and appointed by God, Jesus also felt the rejection of men. He was even rejected by His own countrymen. The bible speaks of a particular time when Jesus had finished teaching the multitude before departing to his own country, and upon his arrival, His own relatives and people refused to accept him for who He was—*The Son of the Living God.*

Now it came to pass, when Jesus had finished these parables, that He departed from there. When He had come to His own country, He taught them in their synagogue, so that they were astonished and said, "Where did this Man get this wisdom and these mighty works? "Is this not the carpenter's son? Is not His mother called Mary? And His brothers James, Joses, Simon and Judas? "And His sisters, are they not all with us? Where then did this Man get all these things?" So they were offended at Him. But Jesus said to them, "A prophet is not without honor expect in his own country and in his own house." Now He did not do many mighty works there because of their unbelief.

(Matthew 13:53-58)

His own people found it extremely hard to accept Him for who He was; maybe because they had known Him from the time He was born up until the time He entered into His ministry. They knew Him as the carpenter's son rather than the Messiah that was born Savior of the world. This reason was enough for His people to deny Him. *"He came to His own, and His own did not receive Him"* **(John 1:11)**.

Even authorities and rulers in high places rejected Jesus.

Then the officers came to the chief priests and Pharisees, who said to them, "Why have you not brought Him?" The officers answered, "No man ever spoke like this Man!" Then the Pharisees answered them, "Are you also deceived? "Have any of the rulers or the Pharisees believed in Him? "But this crowd that does not know the law is accursed." Nicodemus (he who came to Jesus by night, being one of them) said to them, "Does our law judge a man before it hears him and knows what he is doing?" They answered and said to him, "Are you also from Galilee? Search and look, for no prophet has arisen out of Galilee.

(John 7:45-52)

The reason these men rejected Jesus was based on two factors:

1. If the Pharisees and rulers (who were considered to be the holy of the holiest) did not believe in Jesus, why should the rest of the people believe?

2. No prophet has ever risen out of Galilee

Of course, these were the lies the devil used to his advantage for the Pharisees and the rulers to reject the Messiah, and to stop them from inheriting salvation. On the other hand, the rejections that Jesus experienced were all in accordance to the will of God—*"But first He must suffer many things and be rejected by this generation"* **(Luke 17:25)**. Isaiah also wrote, *"He is despised and rejected by men"* **(Isaiah 53:3)**.

On many occasions Jesus found Himself being rejected. On one particular Sabbath day for example, Jesus was in the synagogue and read from the book of Isaiah . . .

The Spirit of the LORD is upon Me, Because He has anointed Me To preach the gospel to the poor; He has sent Me to heal the brokenhearted, To proclaim liberty to the captives and recovery of sight to the blind, To set at liberty those who are oppressed; To proclaim the acceptable year of the LORD.

(Luke 4:18-19)

After Jesus had closed the book and taken His seat, we learnt that He spoke further on the subject and the scriptures. But the Jews became very angry and attempted to throw Him off the cliff.

So all those in the synagogue, when they heard these things, were filled with wrath, and rose up and thrust Him out of the city; and they led Him to the brow of the hill on which their city was built, that they might throw Him down over the cliff. Then passing through the midst of them, He went His way.

(Luke 4:28-30)

This all occurred because men could not find it in themselves to accept Jesus for who He was. However, all these rejections led to the birth of one of the most famous lines in the bible . . .

The stone which the builders rejected Has become the chief cornerstone. This was the Lord's doing; It is marvelous in our eyes.

(Psalms 118:22-23)

No one really wants to experience rejection, and though it may seem like a hard thing to embrace, know that in the things of God, this could prove to be much necessary. Supposing Joseph wasn't rejected by his brothers and casted into the pit? Would he have reigned as the governor over Egypt? Joseph not only preserved his own life, but the seventy people that soon settled in Egypt by his hand, as well as many others that came to Egypt to buy grain.

Now these are the names of the children of Israel who came with Jacob; Reuben, Simeon, Levi and Judah; Issachar, Zebulun and Benjamin; Dan, Naphtali, Gad, and Asher. All those who were descendants of Jacob were seventy persons (for Joseph was in Egypt already).

(Exodus 1:1—5)

Joseph said to them, "Do not be afraid, for am I in the place of God? "But as for you, you meant evil against me; but God meant it for good, in order to bring it about as it is this day to save many people alive. **(Genesis 50:19-20)**

If this is the will of God and we find ourselves going through such reproaches and sufferings, let us rather give God the glory based on these scriptures:

But let none of you suffer as a murderer, a thief, an evildoer, or as a busybody in other people's matters. Yet if anyone suffers as a Christian, let him not be ashamed, but let him glorify God in this matter.

(1 Peter 4:15-16)

The bible even reveals that God the Father was indeed rejected by men. Israel requested for a man to be ruler over them as king. God spoke to Samuel saying—*'for they have not rejected you, but they have rejected Me'* **(1 Samuel 8:7).**

Then all the elders of Israel gathered together and came to Samuel at Ramah, and said to him, "Look, you are old, and your sons do not walk in your ways. Now make us a king to judge us like all the nations." But the thing displeased Samuel when they said, "Give us a king to judge us." So Samuel prayed to the LORD. And the LORD said to Samuel, "Heed the voice of the people in all that they say to you; for they have not rejected you, but they have rejected Me, that I should not reign over them.

(1 Samuel 8:4-7)

Once God has called you for greater works, it doesn't matter how things look in the physical, even if men reject you. God, who is faithful, will accept you according to his purpose. Remember, Gideon was a man from the weakest clan in Manasseh, and the least in his father's house. Maybe if the question was ever to come up in a discussion—'*Which tribe could go up and save us*?', Gideon's tribe would have never been considered, perhaps laughed at. But the Angel who appeared to Gideon rather revealed that he was in fact accepted for the job.

Then the LORD turned to him and said, "Go in this might of yours, and you shall save Israel from the hand of the Midianites. Have I not sent you?" So he said to Him, "O my Lord, how can I save Israel? Indeed my clan is the weakest in Manasseh, and I am the least in my father's house."

(Judges 6:14:15)

Walter Elias (Founder of *Walt Disney*), was a Christian and in his lifetime experienced a stream of rejection from men. At the age of sixteen he had dropped out of school to join the army but unfortunately was rejected for being underage. After considering which career to embark on, Walter pursued a career as a newspaper artist drawing political caricatures or comic strips. It was said that he was fired by a newspaper editor because '*he lacked imagination and had no good ideas*'. After this he went bankrupt several times before he built Disneyland. In fact, the proposed park was rejected by the city of Anaheim on the grounds that it would only attract riffraff. However, Disneyland officially opened on July 18th 1955 and today is considered the greatest theme park in the entire world. Suppose Mr. Elias was never rejected in his newspaper career, would Disneyland ever exist? Would he have ever earned millions of dollars in his lifetime?

Men will reject, but God's gift of greatness in the life of a believer can never be denied.